Time to Play in Early Childhood Education

5
05

i

}

Time to Play in
Early Childhood Education

Tina Bruce

Hodder & Stoughton

A MEMBER OF THE HODDER HEADLINE GROUP

British Library Cataloguing in Publication Data

Bruce, Tina
  Time to play: In early childhood education.
  I. Title
  370.15

  ISBN 0-340-53878-3

First published 1991
Impression number   13 12 11 10 9 8 7 6
Year   1999 1998 1997 1996

Typeset by Litho Link Limited, Welshpool, Powys, Wales.
Printed in Great Britain for Hodder & Stoughton Educational, a division of Hodder Headline Plc, 338 Euston Road, London NW1 3BH by Redwood Books, Trowbridge, Wiltshire

Contents

Dedication

My childhood was drenched with free-flow play. I dedicate this book to my family, with deep thanks. To my parents, Margery and Peter Rowland, and to my brother Marc, as well as my cousins, Daphne and Helen.

'For I was so much older then,
I'm younger than that now.'

Bob Dylan

Acknowledgments

My thanks to Joan Tamburrini and James Willig with whom I had the privilege to study. To Chris Athey, Vendla König and Moira McKenzie for deeply influencing times turning theory into practice. Thanks to Jill Redford, Principal of the Froebel Institute College, Rory Hands, Chair of the Froebel Council, and Phil Robinson, Dean of the School of Education at Roehampton Institute for understanding my need to have time to play with my family.

Thanks to so many people for fascinating conversations about play including Lynne Bartholomew and staff, Anne Findlay, Shirley Maxwell, Helen McAuley, Joyce French, Margy Whalley and staff, Gina Houston, Patricia Juanette and staff, Sheena Johnstone and colleagues at Moray House, the EYCG (Early Years Curriculum Group), Jeni Riley and colleagues at the Institute of Education, University of London, Eve Boyd, Cynthia James, Jill Wiles.

I am grateful to Pat Gura and all the Blockplay Project participants who were so understanding of my prior commitment to write this book, and my concern that it should be kept separate from the book we have written together.

Thanks to the following for their practical help. To Margaret Sargent for her sensitive approach to the photography. To the Etheridge and Vaughan families for helping to feed and entertain the Bruce family whilst I wrote, and to Helena, Catie, Pam and Rosangela, the team of Mothers' helps who have supported the Bruce family and helped the free-flow play to flourish over the years.

To Liz Rowland and Sheila Boyce for getting the manuscript under control and typed, and Kate Mann who helped me so much before she so tragically died. To Diana Simon, Kathy Havekin and Jo Gregson-Williams at Hodder and Stoughton who have been so supportive with the books I have written.

Lastly, Tom, Hannah and Ian, for the family times full of play. Special thanks to Ian, my husband, who gives me courage, goes to endless trouble so that I can write, and asks such difficult questions in such a helpful way.

July 1991   Tina Bruce

The author and publishers would also like to thank the following for permission to reproduce items in this book: Palm Press, Inc. Massachusetts for the photograph on page 126; Little, Brown and Company, Boston for illustrations on pp 121 and 135.

Every effort has been made to trace copyright holders of material reproduced in this book. Any right not acknowledged here will be acknowledged in subsequent printings if notice is given to the publishers.

Introduction

The seeds of the past are there to create the future, whatever we do (Tony Jarman 1989).

We talk about the wisdom that comes with age. We hear elderly people say (a little wearily at times), 'I've seen it all before'. They have lived long enough to know that as we move through our lives, we catch glimpses of how we came to be the person we are today.

Similarly, looking at some of the past and current influences on our work with young children can be a valuable catalyst in this process of metacognition. This means that we come to reflect, to analyse our thinking, to question ourselves, and to seek out whether we agree with ourselves, and what we want to do next. Through this process, we see how consistent we are, how much coherence we achieve. It helps us to move towards our ideals, because we find the direction we would like to take which is right for now, and right for the future. It helps us to operate with more than a pragmatic response to the here and now. When we are purely pragmatic, we have no sense of direction.

At the introductory celebrations of the Commonwealth Games in New Zealand in 1989, the Maori dancers sang, 'Let us know you as you were in times gone by. Let us know you as you are. Let us know you as you dream to be'.

This book is about finding the direction that we want to take in relation to one area of the early years curriculum – that is, what we think free-flow play can contribute to the young child's learning and development. It is also about the way we can translate into practice what we want for young children.

In doing this, we shall need to consider what is free-flow play, but also to look at the processes which interweave, inter-relate and form a network with it. It will become apparent, as we move through the book, that there is great difficulty in using the umbrella term 'play'. The focus needs to be refined so that we can establish what is meant by this word. Many things called 'play' by those of us working with children are not so. Gardner (1982) and the Hutts (1990) point out the difficulties of using the term 'play' indiscriminately.

It is best, therefore, to use adjectives to describe the focus given to play. This book uses Göncü's phrase (1987) 'free-flow play', which links it most closely with imaginative, free or creative play.

In Chapter 4 we shall establish the features of free-flow play, and an equation which explains its essence. I have to confess that if I had my way, nothing else would be referred to as play. In this way, play would become a smaller and more manageable concept. However, it has to be recognised that no-one can be a David figure taking on Goliath, and so it is likely that terms such as 'pleasure play', 'discovery play', 'structured play', 'guided play', 'learning through play', will continue in use. However, I do not see the processes of struggle, manipulation, firsthand experience, practice, games, humour or representation as play, in the strict and pure sense we shall apply to free-flow play. These are different from free-flow play, but they are also invaluable and necessary to the learning process. They form part of the inter-connected network of processes, of which free-flow play is one. Vygotsky (1978, p. 101) suggests, 'play is not the predominant feature of childhood, but it is a leading factor in development'.

Free-flow play has a central part to contribute, and so have all the other processes in this network. Struggle is central, so is exploring and discovering. Firsthand experience is crucial; using what is learnt from it is part of free-flow play. Games help children to understand external pressures and constraints; free-flow play helps children to see the function of rules for themselves, and to design, use and alter rules with sensitivity towards themselves and others. They create, innovate and imagine in free-flow play. Humour makes use of the deepest levels of understanding and knowledge, and lightens the seriousness of free-flow play, games and representation. Humour makes learning deeply satisfying after the struggling, exploring and prac-tising. Representation, where processes and products deve-lop, becomes richer if children have wallowed in ideas, feelings and relationships in an organic and unpressured way, through the process of free-flow play, which has no products. Representation is richer if competence and technical prowess have been applied in the play context. All these processes are of fundamental importance in learning and development. All relate to, and feed off and into, each other.

This book gives major focus to free-flow play, since, of these central processes, it is probably the least understood – because it is the least tangible. It needs clarification and refining so that it can exert its maximum benefit on the learning and development of children, and perhaps adults too.

In Chapter 1, we look at the principles which form the bedrock of the early childhood traditions (Bruce, 1987) and the three Cs of the curriculum (Bruce, 1988). These are the processes within the child, the context in which the child operates, and the content of what is learnt and understood, i.e. child, context and content.

In Chapter 2, we see the influence of existing theories of play in the broad sense, and why it is necessary to refine the focus by describing it as 'free-flow play' in order to clarify the differences between:

1 'Play versus work' theories.

2 'Play as education' theories, which develop as two distinct strands:
    2.1   The preparation for life approach.
    2.2   Play as an integrating mechanism.

Free-flow play has its highest status when seen as one of the 'play as education' theories. It might be given rather a peripheral place if regarded as a 'play versus work' theory.

Where free-flow play is seen as an integrating mechanism, through which knowledge and understanding, feelings and relationships are used and applied, it is seen as a catalyst to, and beneficiary of, the network of processes – including firsthand experience (struggling, exploring, practising), games, humour and representation.

Where play is emphasised as 'preparation for life' it moves towards being adult dominated, adult preconceived and adult led. It tends to be guided or directly structured by adults, and children do not have much ownership in it; it sits very unhappily with the 10 early childhood principles (Bruce, 1987). Why then has it survived? The major reason is its 'commonsense' attractiveness to adults in general, and parents and lay policy makers in particular. While the 'play as an integrating mechanism' approach is hard to describe, play as 'preparation for life and adulthood' is both simple and flattering. In fact, play as 'preparation for life' is more akin to the games with external rule formats, described in Chapter 6.

'Play as an integrating mechanism' is a more sophisticated approach, and in a sense kills two birds with one stone. Because children are given a large say in it – wallowing in ideas, feelings and relationships, and being able competently to apply their own learning in a voluntary and intrinsically motivated way – they gain what they need now. In this way, children integrate and apply their knowledge in ways appropriate during childhood, and in so doing, also prepare for adult life.

From Chapter 3 onwards, the book follows the approach that free-flow play is an integrating mechanism, which brings together everything learned, and helps children to apply their learning. In this Chapter, we look at major influences on the development of free-flow play in the early childhood curriculum. These include the philosophies of educators such as Froebel, Dewey, McMillan and Isaacs, all of whom pioneered free-flow play. It shows the importance of specialist training colleges, reports such as Plowden (1967) and the Early Years Curriculum Group (EYCG) (1989).

Chapter 4 puts forward 12 features of free-flow play which form its underlying deterministic structure. These are simplified in an equation which expresses the essence of the features:

free-flow play = wallow in ideas, + application of com-
                   feelings and   petence and tech-
                   relationships   nical prowess that
                                         has already been
                                         developed

Chapter 5 gives focus to processes that are prerequisites, and integral, to the network including free-flow play. These are firsthand experiencing through struggling, manipulating, exploring, discovering, and practising. They are all of crucial importance and form the bedrock of free-flow play.

Chapter 6 concentrates on processes developing in syncrony with free-flow play. These include the development of games with rules, humour and representation of experience.

Chapter 7 examines a new theory which supports the valuing of free-flow play in education and gives it high status, with the implications that play is an integrating mechanism. This is known as Chaos Theory and emanates from mathematics.

Chapter 8 looks at how we can assess, evaluate and record free-flow play. In the light of the developments in Chaos Theory, it seems important to value apparently disorderly data and underlying structures, rather than to try to predict specific outcomes of free-flow play. It is also important to bring children in on evaluation, assessment and recording of play.

Chapter 9 looks at ways forward through the three Rs. These are the re-exploration of play, the re-statement through the notion of free-flow play and the re-affirmation of its value for all children in education and care settings, and probably in adult life too. Free-flow play takes a central part in a network of important processes, all of which contribute to the child's learning and development in deep and lasting ways.

1 The Foundations of Education – the foundations of free-flow play

In the first book, *Early Childhood Education* (1987), 10 principles of early childhood education were established as a general framework through which to approach our work with young children. This chapter describes the educational background into which free-flow play is set, comprising those 10 principles and a model of the curriculum through the three Cs (Bruce, 1989). From this chapter, we shall lead into the finer focus of examining the importance of free-flow play during early childhood.

Free-flow play is sometimes called 'imaginative play', 'free play', 'fantasy play', 'pretend play' or 'ludic play'. It is not structured play, guided play, games play, practice play or exploratory play. Because we cannot do justice to free-flow play in isolation, away from the network of processes in which it operates, we shall also look at inter-related processes of struggle, exploration, practice, games, representation and humour, as we move through the book.

However, first we need to set the scene for free-flow play through the 10 principles, and through the curriculum model of the three Cs.

The Principles of Early Childhood Education

1   Childhood is seen as valid in itself, as a part of life and not simply as preparation for adulthood. Thus education is seen similarly as something of the present and not just preparation and training for later.

2   The whole child is considered to be important. Health, physical and mental, is emphasised, as well as the importance of feelings, thinking and spiritual aspects.

3   Learning is not compartmentalised, for everything links.

4   Intrinsic motivation, resulting in child-initiated, self-directed activity, is valued.

5   Self-discipine is emphasised.

6   There are specially receptive periods of learning at different stages of development.

7   What they can do (rather than what they cannot do) is the starting point in the child's education.

8   There is an inner structure in the child, which includes the imagination, which emerges especially under favourable conditions.

9   The people (both adults and children) with whom the child interacts are of central importance.

10 The child's education is seen as an interaction between the child and the environment the child is in – including, in particular, other people and knowledge itself (Bruce 1987).

The Three Cs of the Early Childhood Curriculum

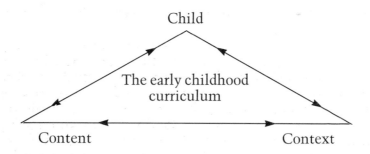

Child

The early childhood curriculum

Content

Context

What the child already knows

What the child needs to know

What the child wants to know more about

People, culture, race, gender, special educational needs, access, materials and physical environment, outdoors, indoors, places, events

The different strands of the early childhood curriculum – the child, the context and the content – are useful analytical tools to help us achieve a holistic curriculum. Over-concentration on any one element (normally the content) will lead to narrowness and lack of balance. Western Europe is not comfortable with holistic approaches, which are common elsewhere. Sandip Hazareesingh (ed. 1989, p. 8) writes:

> Holistic philosophies have long been prominent in Indian, Chinese and African civilisations (as the Indian Spring Festival of Holi, the Chinese spiritual philosophy of Tao).

The holistic approach towards early childhood education is also emphasised in principle number 2. 'The whole child is considered to be important. Health, physical and mental, is emphasised, as well as the importance of feelings and thinking and spiritual aspects.' Having emphasised the importance of a holistic approach to the curriculum, it is still vital to understand the component parts. The remainder of this chapter looks at each of the three Cs in detail. The whole is more than the sum of the parts.

The child

We need to know as much as possible about how children learn and develop.

Matthew, two years, is banging with his hands on a toy drum. The adult gives him a drumstick. Matthew is supported in his knowledge that drums are struck and that you can use hands, but is introduced to the idea of striking with drumsticks in a way that does not break the drum. Once Matthew is banging on the drum with drumsticks, the adult introduces the woodwork bench and shows him how to use a hammer. Matthew can still use what he knows of banging, but with a medium that is unfamiliar. The curriculum offered needs to match Matthew's development, so that he can be supported in what he already knows (drumsticks and trajectories) and also extended into the unknown (trajectories with hammers).

Teaching is one step ahead, as it were, of the child. 'Recent research indicates that more effective learning occurs when the teaching material is pitched at such a level

Trajectory (banging) can be used in familiar ways or extended into new functions.

that is demanding but still within the learner's reach' (Willig, 1990, p. 16). Free-flow play, which is not dominated by adults, facilitates this because children create a setting where they operate at their highest levels of functioning. The observant adult will recognise from this what knowledge the child has gained, and can build on this to introduce the less familiar.

For example, in free-flow play, Matthew (four years) pretending to be in a pop group uses everything he has learnt about drumming. He is free from pressure to perform and imagines he is on stage as a professional adult drummer. He sings a song he makes up as he drums, 'boo boo boom, boo boo boom'. He wallows in ideas about drumming, tunes and performances. He uses his latest techniques without any particular goal. He ends in a flourish, bows to an imaginary audience and leaves.

In their free-flow play, children give us strong signals and messages about what they need now and what they will need next. Matthew, for example, is showing us his interest in banging/hammering, which can be extended into other contexts; his vertical trajectories which can be developed. Unless we match our teaching techniques to the child's learning and development, we cannot support or extend the child's education.

Because this book is looking at free-flow play, it is inevitable that it will focus on the child, because play is a process in the child. However, it is heavily influenced by context. It is therefore most accurate to refer to 'the child-in-context'.

Ask the children about free-flow play perhaps, they know more than adults

In Swedish, the words 'teaching' and 'learning' are the same (Gunni Karrby, 1989, p. 3). This overcomes the problem that what we attempt to teach children may not be what they learn. Having one word brings the two closer together. In a study (1989, p. 4) at the University of Gothenburg, Gunni Karrby and colleagues emphasised the importance of metacognition in young children. In interviews with five-to six-year-old children, the team asked them to reflect on their own thinking about what play is and is not. (In Sweden, formal schooling begins at seven years.)

Generally, children were able to recount, describe and explain in a richer way what had happened during free play than during structured situations. The team found a subworld they had not been able to discover from their direct observations of children during free-flow play, such as the kissing play mentioned later in this chapter. Their findings indicate why it is that most researchers in the 1970s and 1980s stressed the importance of structured, guided activities, rather than free-flow play. Quite simply, it is much easier for adults to study (Clark, 1988). Researchers tend to move in and out of classrooms and are rarely with children continuously. They are also inevitably anxious to demonstrate the scientific rigour of their study.

When looking at the structured play activities, the team at Gothenburg report (p. 4):

> We could easily define the educational setting, and the teachers' intention. However, in the free-flow play setting, we found that we had often misinterpreted the child's own experiences, thoughts and motives.

We can see, viewing the situation from the adults' perspective, that studying free-flow play is a researcher's nightmare. It is understandable that those researching play would focus on that which it is possible to define, identify and easily act upon within the traditional approaches of classical, scientific method.

In the Oxford Studies, Bruner expressed consensus with the Tizards and the Hutts (1980, p. 203) when he wrote of the 'received wisdom' amongst nursery teachers and nursery nurses and playgroup leaders: the 'extraordinary dogmatism' that free-flow play is beneficial to young children. However, in Pascal's study (1990), although teachers in early reception classes talked about prioritising play, their classroom practice did not reflect its translation into active encouragement of this. It may be that those working constantly and directly with young children, and trained to value free-flow play, intuitively recognise that young children are in need of it, but need to feel more confident about actively promoting it. Clark (1988) suggests that early years teachers are not regarded with status by colleagues teaching older children.

Later in this book, we shall look at a new and highly respected scientific theory which may help us to be rigorous and confident in researching and encouraging free-flow play. It is called the Chaos Theory. It may help those of us working directly with the young to justify our intuitions that free-flow play is good for children, and to have courage in helping children to play; thus making it central to education not just in theory, but in practice too. Early years teachers seem almost to have lost their nerve over the last 20 years. The research *TES* (12.10.90), which has gained most publicity, has given the message that free-flow play is not all that it has traditionally been cracked up to be (Bennett and Kell, 1987, p. 7). Fortunately, to experience it with children is to sense it has to be a 'good thing'. Perhaps we should let the children themselves lead us back to have courage to value free-flow play overtly and without hesitancy. As Glenda Bissex says (1980), 'We need to trust the teacher that is in the child'.

Children value play

Gunni Karrby and her colleagues found that children do value free-flow play (p. 5).

> The children thus differentiate play from other activities that are often called 'play' by adults. For children, play is a complex mental activity, not easily observed and interpreted by parents, teachers and researchers.

In other words, play is a creative process. One girl (five to six years) said, 'In fantasy activity, you have to think for yourself'.

Glenda Bissex says that adults must learn to trust the teacher that is in the child. Vivian Gussin Paley's classroom observations support this. The Swedish research shows us that we must see the learner and the teacher as different sides of the same (that we need to get closer together), and that children know free-flow play is good for them. They also recognise that other experiences are good for them, but in a different way.

Gunni Karrby found that children see the more directly structured activities as 'me learning', in the sense of making constructions, mastering bike riding, doing what the teacher wants, and using the teacher's knowledge as a resource to help in the learning of new things. They see these as 'secluded' and separate activities, and want them to be short. In contrast, children see free-flow play as a holistic and integrated event, with group themes, roles, and using their own ideas in a collective atmosphere. They need acres of time for it.

These children are aware that they need to be given opportunities for original, creative and innovative thinking and feeling with others, which is the essence and unique contribution of free-flow play. It is the means by which they not only take their places in society, but contribute to it, with vision, imagination and competence. In Chapter 2, we see that all work and no play makes for dullness.

Susan Ditchburn (1989), University of Calgary, writes, 'It is clear that the teacher is of essence a learner, and conversely that the child is a teacher'. If we listen to children, we shall not so seriously undervalue free-flow play. And if those of us working with young children combine listening to children with trusting our intuitions, using our framework of principles and seeking sound theory and research, we shall also have the courage to value free-flow play and to become catalysts for its occurrence.

The context

It is through the context of the education setting, and the people the child meets, that access to the curriculum is gained. We saw at the beginning of the chapter that the context includes people, culture, race, gender, special educational needs, materials and physical environment, indoor and outdoor settings, places, and events.

All these are crucial in enabling or constraining access to both learning and development, and so to education. The child with a visual impairment, the child brought up in a Sikh community, the child in a house with no books, the child who is regularly taken to borrow library books, the child who is abused, the only child, the child in bed-and-breakfast accommodation, the child with a nanny, the child who lives in an extended family, the child whose home has a swimming pool, the child who has no breakfast, the child who is bilingual – all these factors have an impact and an influence on the child's access to education, and to play in particular.

The issues surrounding 'context', and the ways that access to play is empowered, constrained or denied, are crucial. An essential aspect of the child's context is having access to it. Without full access, the context, however rich it is, may as well not exist. It needs to be on offer, but it also needs to be possible for the child to be able and wanting to make full use of it. Issues of access are particularly important in relation to gender, race, culture, special educational needs, poverty of environment, and people as catalysts. Whether the people the child encounters are catalysts or not will have the greatest impact on full access to the curriculum.

People

When a child first joins a care or education group of any kind (e.g. child-minder, playgroup, workplace nursery or nursery school), both the parents and those working with the child are important influences.

Parents as partners

In embracing the child's cultural background, it would not make sense to try to educate a child without taking account of the most significant people in his/her environment, and trying to work with them. It is through the home context that school becomes meaningful, or not, to a family. Whether or not parents have the same ideas about 'play' is going to be crucial. The way parents and professionals develop shared meanings about play is explored throughout the book, because it is one of the most critical issues in determining what kind of access children have to a complete education.

People who work with young children need to bear in mind that the child's best educational interests are not served by negative undertones, which criticise the attitudes of parents towards free-flow play. We do not want to sit in judgement of families, we need to develop some shared strategies and shared understandings about 'free-flow play' so that we can work together, from the starting-point of the family. Alice Honig (1984) stresses the importance of building our observational skills together. Davenport (1943) points out the different emphasis of different cultures, through observing the different attitudes to play in the Sikh children she taught. Minnie Kumria (1986) reiterates this need for sharing thoughts and information.

When parents and teachers tune into each other and think about free-flow play, important things begin to happen. Professionals become careful about beginning from the family's viewpoint, and have to develop good self-esteem about themselves and what they believe in. They, like parents, need to value themselves, and their work with children. Neither the role of parents, nor that of those educating and caring for young children, has high status in Britain, and the problem is made worse by research studies on play during the 1970s and 1980s which were critical towards those working directly with young children (Tizard and Hughes, 1984; Hutt, 1990; Oxford Studies, 1980; and Bennett, 1989).

This has contributed to a serious undermining of confidence amongst early years professionals, of their intuitive knowledge that free-flow play is important for young children. It has always been difficult to articulate what those close to young children sense is good for them, and these research studies have not furthered their ability to find a voice for free-flow play. Instead, influential research has tended to question its value. It seems that both parents and professionals have precarious self-esteem. If both feel good about the way they interact with young children, it is easier for truly reciprocal relationships to develop. It is therefore urgent that we look again at free-flow play, to see if the intuitions of the early childhood traditions described (Lesley Webb, 1974) have validity, and that free-flow play is of true value in the young child's education.

Understandably, parents tend to focus on the products of what children do, because these are tangible. We could call it the 'Have you done a painting today?' syndrome. The teacher who shares the continuous and formative observations of the child at play will be more able to help the parent see the relationship between processes without product, such as play, and the processes that have personal or shareable products, as in representation.

For example, Barbara (three years) made a house at home. She was allowed to rearrange the furniture, making walls out of the sofa and chairs. She made a bedroom, kitchen, bathroom and living room, and played houses. Her mother told the teacher. The teacher suggested that she might be using her understanding of space through the Piagetian schema (Bruce, 1987; Athey, 1990) of an enclosure, divided and partitioned. The whole room was an enclosure, divided into smaller enclosures. The parent pointed out a drawing Barbara had done that week, which was just that. She said the drawing was a house with rooms. Barbara's mother could see the relationship between free-flow play and representation, and valued both.

Cultural background and race

Sandip Hazareesingh (*et al.*, 1989, p. 37) defines the child's cultural identity as, 'whatever a child finds to be emotionally meaningful and significant – both about himself/ herself and in his/her life'. Any approach which strives to begin with the child, needs to begin with the child's culture.

Sandip Hazereesingh also states (p. 24):

> Meaningful learning can only occur if what the child brings in terms of concrete experiences is seen by the teacher as the essential component of his/her planning of the curriculum and in the (resource-based) organisation of the classroom environment.

Every area of provision needs to be considered in relation to the child's culture, e.g. Penny Lewis (1988, p. 36), writes:

> The home corner has immense potential as a place where children can learn constructively about themselves and others, and learn respect for those practices which are different from their own.

Jane Miller (1983) points out that more than 50 per cent of the world's population is bilingual, and so are 15 per cent of London's schoolchildren.

Playing together (e.g. in the home corner, as Penny Lewis describes) gives children opportunities to use language in an active, functional and comprehensive setting. It helps children to communicate across languages and cultures. It needs adults who value diversity of both, and who show this in the way they resource and help children to use the play opportunities the classroom offers. When we look at free-flow play, it is important to remember that it is often our unwitting actions and attitudes which do most damage. Without intending to do so, it is easy to ignore the child's culture and render it 'silenced and invisible' (Sandip Hazareesingh, 1989, p. 24).

Sukvinder (three years) joined her teacher in the home corner. She said 'girl' and pointed to herself. She found a Sikh costume. She smiled when she put it on, deeply satisfied. She identified with being Asian, and this was valued in the home corner. When we do something as simple as giving a baby a rattle, we take part in a cultural event. The setting up of resources which children can make use of in free-flow play is of central importance in tackling unwitting racism.

Gender

When children play, they try out the different roles and relationships they have learned about. In Spielberg's film, 'Always' (1990), the hero gives his girlfriend what she calls 'girl clothes' for her birthday – pink, fluffy and shimmering, with high-heeled shoes. Studies (ed., Gura directed by Bruce in press, 1992) show typical gender differences in children's play. Boys are found in the block area, on tricycles, outdoors, at construction areas, etc. Girls are found in dolls houses in the home corner, sitting at table activities and wearing tutus and high heels.

There have been various attempts towards gender equality, in breaking down socially restrictive gender roles.

(a) Sandip Hazareesingh (*et al.*, 1989, p. 38) offers 'boys and girls equally active and exploring, as well as tender and nurturing, roles'. Roles can be broadened by giving boys dolls (e.g. He-man or Action man) and girls construction kits (e.g. Lego with flowerpots or other 'home' type elements).

(b) There can be girls-only sessions on the bikes and boys-only sessions in the home corner. There is a problem here in that girls are usually quite able to negotiate with other girls to get bikes and boys collaborate well with each other in the home corner, but difficulties arise when girls negotiate with boys to have a turn on the bikes, or boys with girls in the house.

(c) One of the most helpful strategies seems to be for the adult to join the party (bikes, home corner, blocks, dolls houses, etc.) without dominating it, and to be a catalyst to both boys and girls, gaining access and broadening their roles and experiences (Gura, ed., directed by Bruce in press, 1992).

It is important that both girls and boys have access to different kinds of free-flow play in the fullest way. Culture, race, languages, family, gender, and people are all facets that contribute to the child's access to free-flow play.

Girls tend to be regarded as good students more often than boys in the early years of education, but they may not be developing the spatial concepts necessary for the high-level mathematics of the secondary school (Dunn and Morgan, 1987). They may need to free-flow play in a more expansive way, as the boys tend to do when involved in rough-and-tumble play or tearing round the playground on tricycles. Early childhood education is about giving both boys and girls access to the curriculum, and free-flow play is an important part of that.

At school, a group of five year olds play princes and princesses. They are doing a medieval project, and the teacher has told them about the Black Prince. At playtime, Hannah asks if she can dress up in a princess costume. The teacher says, yes. Rufus and James put on costumes – one is the Black Prince, the other a knight. (There is also a feeling of King Arthur about it – James is Sir Lancelot.) Hannah dashes away and the boys give chase. James is to rescue Hannah if Rufus captures her. Other girls join in, hoping and not hoping to be captured by Rufus. There are peals of laughter, and the teacher goes for coffee.

In Sweden, Gunni Karrby (1989) found that six-year-old children, when asked about their free-flow play, began to explain a kissing play between boys and girls. It identified a subworld unknown to adult observers. Perhaps rather than being simply sex-stereotyped play, chase with kisses – or with princes and princesses – in a free-flow playstyle is an important means of access for both boys and girls, in entering together the rowdy and boisterous play which children need.

Special educational needs

A teacher at a school for physically disabled children attended a 10-week inservice course for early years teachers in mainstream settings at the Froebel Institute College, RIHE. She wanted to look at how the able-bodied child engages in free-flow play, in order to reflect and act upon specific resources that might be needed. She felt that the children she taught were losing out, and were further handicapped in their disability because they could not engage in such play. It is important to distinguish between the physical impairment of a child, which is a medical condition and concerns the areas of difficulty in leading a normal life, and the handicap which is often caused by lack of resources, facilities or imaginative sensitivity by others. Roy McConkey (Smith, 1986, p. 106) argues that, 'No group needs these outcomes (play) more than children born with, or who acquire, physical, mental, emotional or social disabilities'. As a result, the teacher developed the home corner, so that children could choose props and hold objects. She emphasised stories and interest tables which gave opportunities to explore, struggle and practise using these. She realised that the curriculum she offered emphasised structured activities, life skills and games requiring matching, for example, matching a cup to a picture of a cup, or finding two identical pictures. Everything involved carrying out adult-set goals and tasks. She needed to give children opportunities to choose, and to signal their own ideas, so that she could help them to play, and to 'own' their developing knowledge.

For example, having a play picnic, with cups, etc., on a mat on the floor made it easier for Thomas (six years) to grab and reach objects and pretend to eat, as he did not have to concentrate on using his callipers. Lack of such free-flow play opportunities would mean that he would be subjected to double delay, through both his disability and the handicap of lack of access to the curriculum (Neilsson, 1985).

The physical environment

The National Children's Home fact file, *Children in Danger* (1990), states that families on income support do not have enough money to give their young children a nutritious diet, and how this 'points to widening disparities in services and general well-being between different areas of the country and different types of families'. Malcolm Wicks (VOLCUF, AGM, 1989) reports that a quarter of families with children under five are now on the poverty line. Children on a poverty-induced poor diet, in poor housing – e.g. bed and breakfast accommodation where they cannot be noisy, busy and dangerous streets, isolation in rural areas, high-rise flats without gardens – all make free-flow play less accessible for young children. Only 23 per cent of children in Great Britain attend nursery schools and classes: 'Facilities in the maintained sector accommodate a substantially higher proportion of disadvantaged children than is found in the independent sector' (Osborn and Milbank, 1987, p. 240).

LEA institutions accept more children with handicaps, behavioural problems and delayed development than play-groups. However, two in four children receive no nursery education of any kind, and many of these are families under stress. Osborn and Milbank point to the success of nursery schools, argue that all children benefit from nursery education, and advocate its expansion. 'Access to education has already become unequal for young children by the time they reach the statutory age for starting school' (Clark, 1988, p. 277).

This means that only some children are gaining full access to free-flow play in its richest possibility, despite the continuous recommendations of researchers and government-appointed committees that nursery education benefits children's learning and development. Britain now has the worst record in this area in Western Europe (Moss, 1989).

Outdoor areas and the early childhood curriculum

If children are denied opportunities to move physically in their free-flow play their education is constrained. In many inner-city areas, the community is joining with schools to create exciting and enabling outdoor play areas. Children need to climb, run, jump, and bash balls against high walls (Lewis Howdle, lecture, RIHE, 1980). They need trees, although climbing frames help. They need flowers, gardens, areas for bikes and trucks, areas for dens, and hoses to spray.

Children play a few yards from their home, whether it has dangerous traffic or not. This has led to the development of safe-play streets near the front doors – rather than playgrounds away from the houses, which are not as useful for little children. Free-flow play is ideally in the heart of the community, and in the child's home, school or care setting (Naylor, in Smith, 1986).

Indoor areas and access to free-flow play

The area needs to be resourced, organised, managed and aesthetically arranged, so that what it offers for free-flow play is developmentally appropriate (NAEYC, 1987). The reality is that beauty often has to be created from squalor

(HMI, Report on School Buildings) on a shoestring budget.

The heart of the community may be the playgroup, but whilst supporting playgroups, Lady Plowden also wants to see a nursery school in every area, since this acts as a catalyst for excellence (Evidence to the Select Committee Report on Provision for Under Fives, 1989). Osborn and Milbank's research (1987) and the report of the Rumbold Committee (1990) also stress the importance of provision provided by local authorities in serving the needs of communities.

The content

We have seen in the sections on the child, and on the context that it is essential to the sound teaching of content, that adults know and understand both how children develop and the context in which they develop. As John Matthews says (1987, p. 181), 'this requires that teachers be enlightened as to the nature of the child's internal programme', and, as Wynne Harlen points out (1982), that they have at their disposal a 'possible line of direction' for the subject content to take.

It is not the intention, in considering content in the curriculum, to grind through the subjects of the National Curriculum – since through a curriculum emphasising free-flow play, it is expected that children will go far beyond the NC's minimal requirements. Emphasising free-flow play leads to an equal valuing of science and dance, of mathematics and art, of English and drama, of technology, design and music, of geography and history, to give a few examples. In this chapter, the aim is to look at the principles behind the teaching of content, rather than to advocate specific content in free-flow play.

How can content, as Lilian Katz (1987) puts it, be both covered and mastered, in ways which stress the value of free-flow play? Mastery of content emphasises that children have a sense of ownership about the content they learn. In free-flow play, children control and master what they have learnt to a greater extent than in any of the other processes of learning and development. That is why it is essential that they have opportunites to operate at this, the highest level of their functioning (Bruce, 1987, Ch. 5).

In free-flow play children can develop their understanding

and knowledge of content without the pressure of having to make an overt product. This is fundamental to original, innovative and creative thinking (Feynman, 1990). Free-flow play also helps them to find ways of using the technical prowess and competence they have struggled and practised to acquire, in relation to particular content. In play, the learned content comes together and integrates into a wholeness of knowledge and understanding. The process of play is a catalyst to children producing overt products of the content learned in representation, humour and games.

Children need to feel ownership of their learning

It is important that children feel ownership of the content they learn. What they learn belongs to them, and not to the adults. Penny Lewis (1988, p. 6), writing about religious education in the early years, believes that:

> An underlying ethic of nursery provision is that the child has considerable control over his/her learning. In other words, learning is seen as rising out of needs and interest of the child, not necessarily always imposed from outside the child's experience.

Lewis also stresses:

> The teacher should be able to identify the religious strands behind the experiences the children are encouraged to explore. Ideas of awe, wonder, joy and mystery do not 'just happen', they need to be built up and developed.

This would apply in the teaching of any subject content, be it religious studies, mathematics or dance, and it can be done in two ways. When adults join children's play sensitively, this becomes possible. For example, Jenny (four years) was looking at a snail in the garden. She was fascinated by its trail. She came to tell the teacher about it. The teacher was mopping the floor. She looked at the wet trail the mop made. A few days later, she noticed Nasreen had made a trail. She was wet on her front after leaving the water tray and she had lain on the floor to retrieve a cup under the table. Jenny was excited. The teacher helped her to put on an apron, and tied a damp sponge on her front. She began to play snails, crawling along on her stomach, leaving a trail. Two children joined her, demanding snail costumes.

A second method is to have a flow chart with 'possible lines of development', as Wynne Harlen suggests, and to select the content from it which best matches the child's current pattern of exploration. In this way, children make use of the experiences we give them, be it firsthand experiences (such as making electric circuits to make the lights go on in the dolls house), or secondhand experiences, using story themes. Aidon Warlow (1977, p. 93) writes that children often use a well-known and loved story to create their own stories, almost as a jumping-off board, but children use firsthand experiences, such as the snails in the garden, as much as literature. David Evans (1978) notes that they also do this in their song writing.

Jacob (four years) sings 'Three Blind Mice' on a long car journey. He asks his parents to sing 'Baa Baa Black Sheep'. He begins to sing 'Three Blind Mice' while they sing it. His parents ask him what he's doing. He says he wanted to see what it sounded like. They sing it again and again. At first it sounds terrible, but gradually, he changes his tune to fit in harmony with 'Baa Baa Black Sheep'. He is composing, free-flow playing, and his long-suffering parents are encouraging him to do so.

Stories give ideas which can be used by children in their spontaneous free-flow play.

It is important that children hear plenty of stories, so that they have ideas they can use for their own. It is also important that this does not become teacher dominated and geared towards 'let's play this story'. (Meadows and Cashdan, 1988, p. 97) Children need to choose their own themes, and to be helped with open-ended suggestions, which they can choose to use or not.

Chris (six years) wanted to make something with different coloured dough. He remembered this activity from a year before when visiting his aunt. At his request, she made red, blue, green and yellow dough. He made a man, paying great attention to the colours of his clothes, and then made the man walk and played with him. The story was rather like the song 'I went to School One Morning and I Jumped Like This'. He controlled the medium, the ideas and the themes in his free-flow play.

David (five years) was struck with the idea of being a fireman. He free-flow played – turning on imaginary hoses, climbing ladders, and running for the fire engine when he sounded the bell (his voice). For Christmas, he was given a fireman's outfit. Adults were responding to his initiatives in free-flow play.

Certainly adults can 'offer' materials, stories and themes, but it is for children to own them, or indeed to be allowed not to take up the offers.

Three mothers took six children between three and five years of age to the zoo. The most popular area was the aquarium. This group of mothers did swaps, so that once a week each had all the children in her own house/flat while the other mothers were given the time off. A few days after this visit, the children were still talking about the poisonous dragon fish. The 'host' mother drew a picture of a fish. 'No', said Wally, 'like this', and he drew his own version. Soon all the children drew dragon fish. Rachel wanted to put hers on the floor, and to make coral and rocks. The mother asked if polystyrene would do. Rachel was interested. The children seized upon the idea, making rocks by breaking off pieces of polystyrene.

PJ then saw newspapers, and tore them up to make shreds of seaweed. To those who do not value free-flow play, the kitchen floor looked grim. To those who do, it had become the sea and the children were bringing in stones and shells from the bowl in the bathroom, and soft toys (e.g. a soft whale, a plastic fish) to put in it. A plastic frog was rejected because it needed fresh water. A penguin was rejected because dragon fish need warm water.

The children sat on the kitchen table and said they were fishing. The mother found string and glued velcrose onto the line and onto the paper fish. People fell overboard, were rescued, swam with dolphins, caught fish, dived, splashed. They ate tea sitting on the boat. When it was time to go home, the children cleared the rubbish into a box – but it was used several times more when the same group of children met.

In this free-flow play, the adult was involved in four things that Gordon Wells (1987, p. 218) believes are essential, and which also support Wynne Harlen and Paul Black (1992, in press) in their work on science in the National Curriculum.

1 Taking what the child says seriously.

2 Trying to understand what the child means.

3 Using the child's meaning as the basis for the adult's next remark or suggestion.

4 Trying to speak or act in a way that the child will understand.

Wells (1983, p. 150) suggests that something like free-flow play should be 'sufficiently open-ended for the relevance of the children's contributions to be negotiated as the talking (play) proceeds'.

John Matthews (1988, p. 165) notes that children move in and out of free-flow play and representation almost imperceptably at times. Whilst painting, a child might represent the movement of the plane, or represent the wings of the plane. This might then move into play, as the child lifts the painting and begins to use it as a prop to play with.

Cathy Nutbrown stresses that children appreciate adults sensitively suggesting materials which help them to play. Both John Matthews and Cathy Nutbrown have used Piagetian schema theory (Athey, 1990) to help them extend both representation and play in young children.

Metacognition and play

Free-flow play does not have to use spoken words; that is one of its great strengths. Inevitably, during the 1970s and 1980s, when educational research emphasising language was dominant, aspects of the curriculum rich in spoken language held status; dance, music, art and P.E. withered in comparison. Gardner (1982, p. 211): writes

> To come to grips with the world of symbols, a world in large part designed by the culture, is the principal challenge of the years following infancy. The most familiar example, of course, is language but equally stunning progress occurs on all other symbolic fronts.

Free-flow play helps children to appreciate both verbally and non-verbally, as Sally Carline's work (1989) suggests. Sometimes we can overdo the talking (Bruce in Gura, ed. 1992, in press).

Using video tapes, Sally Carline shows how children echo movements, and in this way, she suggests partner dances develop. This links with Hartup's insights (1983) into the way young children coordinate gestures and actions in parallel, and how this leads into free-flow play together. Music, movement and drama, in particular, encourage this. For example, during barn dancing in the Ravenscourt Park, Hammersmith, on a Saturday evening, there are as many children echo-dancing around the edges (often two to seven year olds) as there are adults dancing in the centre, and the children are often doing this in syncrony with each other.

The value of the indirectly structured curriculum

We need to remember that pumping content into children does not mean that they learn it. Indeed, most adults find it difficult to remember much of the content they learnt at school.

Vivian Gussin Paley (1986, p. 107) reminds us:

> After many years of teaching I must admit that mine is not the primary voice in the classroom. Only rarely, for example, do my words find their way into children's stories. I may draw attention to the storyteller's ideas, but I remain the commentator, and not the inventor.

The inventions are in the free-flow play of children, which shows us the content that children have come to own – if we decide to help them.

Summary

The chapter began with a reminder of the 10 principles which form the bedrock of early childhood education; and then looked at the three Cs of the early childhood curriculum. We have seen how they form an inter-related network, and that when looking at processes in the child, we inevitably become involved in thinking about the context in which the child lives and learns. It is important to match what we do with children's learning and development in ways which help them to move forward. People, as well as materials, make an essential part of the play context, and access is a central issue. In the last section, we considered how content is best offered to the young child, in relation to free-flow play.

Content teaching cannot occur in a vacuum. It needs to link with the child-in-context. Any subject content takes children into making, doing and appreciating, whether in dance, art or music, or in mathematical, scientific, literary, historical or technological ways. Children need a broad and deep range of content, and free-flow play makes an important contribution to this. It enables children to own their knowledge.

2 Existing Theories of Play

In this chapter, we shall see how existing theories seep into the ways in which each of us views play, even though this is likely to be, and to remain, at an implicit level. It also affects the way researchers approach the study of free-flow play. The chapter covers play, in its broad definition. Subsequent chapters will concentrate on free-flow play and associated activities, rather than play as an umbrella term.

Theories separating work and play

The following two theories lead us to think of work and play as separate activities. This polarisation of work and play has caused great difficulty over the last two hundred years.

1 Recreation theory

This proposes that children should be given a balance between the 'academics' and the 'non-academics' in the curriculum. Play replenishes the energy expended in doing so-called academic work, usually perceived as the three Rs (Spodek, 1983, p. 181; Smilansky, 1969, p. 48, Almy et al. in Katz, 1984, p. 2). It is sometimes used as a reward to children who have 'worked hard' doing things it is imagined they don't like doing, e.g. writing (the 'When you have finished your work, you can play' syndrome).

OMEP, the International Organisation for Children, has recently been involved in the setting up of an International Children's Charter, UNICEF (1989), since many children in the world do not experience childhood as a time when they have opportunities to learn and develop appropriately. This chapter puts forward 'The child's right to play'. Margaret Roberts (opening speech, 1989, Redford House Nursery Froebel College, RIHE) makes the distinction between the child's right to recreation and the child's right to play.

There is often confusion between them, and this caused much debate in setting up the Charter. Throughout the world, it is common to find play and recreation regarded as one and the same.

In Britain, Joyce Watt (1988) points out that parents are doubtful about the value teachers place on giving children opportunities to play during school time, except as a set playtime when they can 'let off steam' and relax. Typically, parents ritualise the start of formal schooling by sending the child off in a uniform and holding a satchel, which preferably contains a reading book. Play is seen as recreation, and surely children are not sent to school for that. Understandably, parents want their children to go to school so that they can learn. This demonstrates that we need to develop shared meanings – simply finding another word for play won't help (Bruce, BPW Conference, 1990).

We know that it is of great importance for children to develop shared meanings as they free-flow play together (Göncü, 1987). Adults also need to develop shared meanings about play. At the moment, typically, parents do not want 'play' in infant/junior schools except at breaktime, because that is seen as recreation, and not learning. They are prepared to tolerate it until the child is about four years old because their child can meet other children and adults beyond the family circle. However, if it is offered, they tend to leap at the opportunity for a place in an infant class at that age where they hope that 'real work' and little play takes place.

HMI (1988) suggests 62 per cent of four year olds are now in infant classes. Pascal (1990) suggests the figure may be as high as 80 per cent, with the prevailing tendency 'To get them in and get them on' (Cleave and Brown, NFER, 1989; Clark, 1988).

Excess energy theory

This derives from Spencer (1872) and was influenced by the 'letting off steam' concept of industrial machinery. Play is seen as an acceptable way for children to do this, e.g. rough-and-tumble play.

Both recreation theory and excess energy theory lead to 'playtime', as separated from 'worktime'. In contrast, the following theories see play as a central part of education.

Theories making play a central part of education

1 Recapitulation theory

This derives from Stanley Hall (1884-1924). Play reflects the culture, and the individual child works through the development of the species, e.g. in play, the child reproduces prehistoric periods of the human race (wandering tribes, hunting, war, the fight for existence, building shelters).

2 Learning through play – practice theory, or preparation theory

Groos (1922) believed that play helps children to prepare for adult life by letting them, in a natural way, practise and explore what they will need to be able to do as adults. More recently, Bruner (1983, p. 43) has seen play as 'preparation for the technical and social life that constitutes human culture'. Bruner's views are looked at in more detail later in the chapter.

This approach usually leads into what is often called 'guided play', 'structured play' or 'learning the play way'; all of which are adult dominated.

3 Pleasure play

Charlotte Buhler (1937) emphasised the pleasure of playing: 'Activity in itself, that is the pure motor activity involved in merely activating the moving parts of the body, is a source of pleasure, and is in no way dependent upon the anticipated results of this activity'.

Although the theories discussed so far are all old theories, they have by no means disappeared, as we have seen. Indeed, the preparation for life theory dominates today.

4 Affective theories of play

The period 1930s–60s is probably most significant for the development of what may be termed 'child-centred' theories of play. Piaget (Swiss) wrote *Play, Dreams and Imitation* in

1945 and this was translated into English in 1951, but was difficult to understand fully in translation: Vygotsky (Russian) writing on play in the 1930s was not translated into English until 1978. Susan Isaacs, although she met Piaget (Gardner, p. 68, 1969) when he visited her school in the 1930s was more in accord with Freud and, later, Melanie Klein. Indeed, it was the psychodynamic theories which had most influence during this period.

These are child-centred theories, in that children are seen to gain control of their lives and to become integrated people through play. Adults and other children act as catalysts to the play.

(a) Freudian Theories

Freud believed play to be a cathartic experience for children. It took them into and out of reality and helped them to feel mastery and control, so that they coped with anxieties and conflicts and also reflected on positive experiences. In this way, play interpreted experience and made the child whole.

Klein believed children could be helped through analysis at a very young age, whereas Anna Freud believed it necessary to wait until the oedipal stage (four to six years), which followed the oral (up to two years) and anal stages (two to four years).

(b) Erikson

According to Erikson, individuals are always partners with their futures (Maier H., 1978, p. 132). During the third of Erikson's eight stages of development, the child (four to six years) 'makes like' and he describes this as the 'play age'. Children need to play both alone and with others. Through play they develop initiative, and become equipped to overcome disappointments, failures, unfulfilled goals, and to approach life with a sense of increasingly focused purpose (p. 107).

Janet Atkin (1988) stresses that the 'as if' element is a central hallmark of free-flow play. In his eight stages of development, Erikson gives 'as if' play a prominent place during childhood. He had asked children to construct exciting scenes based on imaginary movies. He was struck by the way the scenes the children created seemed to serve as metaphors for their lives. Their scenes (or free-flow play) reflected their chief concerns and interests, their goals and fears, and their strengths and weaknesses.

When he visited the children many years later, he found that their adult lifestyles had been implicit in the themes of their childhood play (Erikson, 1977). This led him to the view that in free-flow play children deal with experience by creating model situations through which they master, plan and experiment. Erikson (1963, p. 222) writes that the child 'relives the past and thus relives left-over affects. He anticipates the future from the point of view of a corrected and shared past'. For example, Anthea (nine years) plays with her dolls house. It is lived in by a family, with father and daughter, Flora. The mother has died and a small doll represents a stepmother with four children. Anthea identifies with Flora. Through Flora she expresses and deals with her fears of loss of those she loves and depends upon. She demonstrates her determination that she will survive and make a good life.

(c) Winnicott

In Bruce (1987, p. 71–2), Winnicott's theory of the importance of the transitional object in the development of play is explored through the example of Ellen. Winnicott believes that throughout our lives we can have important relationships with powerful events, hero figures, pieces of music or paintings, which are akin to a transitional object; and play is the means by which we form these relationships. This is because their importance is created by the person and no-one else. They are given sustenance through being owned by us, and merged with what is important to us (1971, p. 36). The continuities between early childhood free-flow play, fantasy in adolescence and creativity in adult life are stressed by Jerome and Dorothy Singer (1990).

5   Cognitive development theories

The child-centred theories we have looked at so far are affective theories. In these theories, free-flow play strategies are important throughout life. Next, we shall look at some *cognitive* developmental theories, which are also child-centred in their approach but which do not emphasise the importance of free-flow play in adult life.

[a] Piaget

Piaget (1951), like Erikson and Winnicott, saw play as the means by which the child unifies experience, knowledge and understanding. Children control these through play, which generally involves using what is already known (assimilation), rather than adjusting to what is not known (accommodation), through the process he calls 'equilibration'.

The balance (the process of equilibration) is always changing, which is why free-flow play is a process and not a steady state. It is a state of becoming, rather than a state of being.

accommodation				assimilation
←				→
struggle	practice	play	humour	bored

Unlike Erikson and Winnicott or the Singers, Piaget sees free-flow play as something that develops into games with rules, rather than regarding free-flow play as developing into drama, literature, dance imagination, creative writing, creative painting, research in science, etc., throughout adult life. He does not separate the distinction between the creative, innovative strand of symbolic play and the prescribed external rules of a game of chess. If he did, he would see free-flow play and games as two different systems, moving in syncrony. Instead, he sees a linear development, which suggests the development of the free-flow aspects of play into the rule behaviour of games.

Piaget has been criticised for the 'cold cognition' (Shirley Cohen, 1968) of his theory, and his undervaluing of the creative arts (Gardner, 1982). However, he made a great contribution by stressing the importance of free-flow play for young children and in demonstrating that children are active in their learning, using play to further their development in cognitive, as well as affective, ways.

Through the 1930s, to the 1960s, the theories discussed above were major influences. There was considerable concensus from the more child-centred cluster of theories, stemming from the psychoanalyic theory and cognitive developmental theory that play is 'a good thing', both at school, in care settings and at home.

(b) Bruner

During the 1960s, the theories of Bruner became widely known to teachers in Great Britain. In 1983, he wrote that the 'increased dominance of play during immaturity among great apes and hominoids serves as a preparation for the technical social life that constitutes human culture (p. 43). Bruner sees language games such as Ride a Cock Horse as part of this, together with games such as Peek-a-boo. Play is seen as games with rule formats, which are a preparation for life. He believes that mammals have long childhoods, as there is much for them to prepare for in adult life.

Whereas Piaget sees free-flow play as developing into games with rules (e.g. chess), Bruner sees play as games from the start, and so does not focus on free-flow play, except to express unease about rough-and-tumble play, sand, clay, water, dough play (which is apparently without aim). He sees these free activities as lacking intellectual challenge or purpose (Bruner, 1980), because in his terms, they are lacking shared rule formats and not conforming to the conventions of behaviour found in the games which prepare children to take their place in society and culture, e.g. Peek-a-boo.

(c) Vygotsky

Although Vygotsky's theories in relation to language and thought were known in Great Britain in the 1960s, his thinking on play, formulated in the 1930s in Russia, was not translated into English until 1978. Whereas Froebel expressed play in terms of it being the most spiritual activity of the child, representing the highest phase of child development, Vygotsky (1978) postulates a 'zone of potential development' created by play. In this zone, the children, like Froebel's children, operate at their highest level of functioning, beyond their present-day capabilities, so that they become a 'head taller' than themselves. He also believes that free-flow play lifts children onto another plane of functioning. Adults and other children can be catalysts in the process.

However, like Piaget, Vygotsky (1978, p. 95) sees play as developing into games with rules: 'Just as the imaginary situation has to contain rules of behaviour, so every game with rules contains an imaginary situation' (e.g. playing shops, or the game of chess). Like Piaget, he sees the imaginary situations leading finally into games with rules – chess, tennis, fencing, dance performance (rather than innovation or dance choreography, musical composition, scientific thought, or play writing). However, like Bruner, he stresses the social relationships essential to this process.

After the age of eight years, Piaget, Vygotsky and Bruner all value games with rules more than they value free-flow play. Piaget and Vygotsky put games with rules at the top of a linear, hierarchical development. Bruner favours games with rules from the start, which he sees developing from the baby's Peek-a-boo game, and is uneasy about situations with no clear format of rules, e.g. the sand tray, or rough-and-tumble play.

6   Affective and cognitive

Susannah Millar (1968) saw play as the opportunity for children to explore the familiar, practise what is already mastered, to be aggressive in a friendly manner, and to be excited about 'nothing'. She thought it gave children the possibility of imitating social behaviour in situations where it had not been called for. In essence, she brought together the affective and cognitive child-centred theories.

The confused impact of these theories on the education system (1950s and 1960s)

From the 1950s onwards, there was sufficient support for the importance of play to encourage educators, gradually and increasingly, to take it as part of the curriculum beyond the nursery school and into primary schools, using psycho-analytic and cognitive development theories as support.

However, as Dearden points out (1968, p. 93):

> The old elementary school was quite clear about play. It had no business there. Children came to school to work, to 'get down to it and no nonsense'. At the most, some brief intermissions of 'playtime' could be allowed, as concessions to animal spirits and as a recuperation for the next bout of work.

In this way, the old elementary or primary school was reflecting the recreation theory and the surplus energy theory. Dearden acknowledges that to view play and work as separate in this way, to see them as work versus amusement, caused concern for those trained in theories supporting the notion of play as education, i.e. the child-centred theories, both affective and cognitive we have explored. As if to overcome the recreation – or surplus energy – approach of separating work from play, there emerged in the child-centred movement a tendency towards a muddled overclaiming for play. Early childhood workers tended to call everything 'play', in an effort to put across the message 'play is a good thing', and to take advantage of the growing reverence for play.

Mellor (1950, p. 20) states:

> The irresistible urge in young children to be active, to investigate and discover, to imitate and pretend, to plan and construct, finds its outlet in what we call play. Play means those activities which are not connected with our work, [1] and which should perhaps be termed recreation. Some of the children's actions are in this category, for example, when he 'lets off steam'; [2] and abandons himself to the sheer delight of movement after a period of concentration; [3] but if we watch children 'at play' we shall see that much of their activity is of a very serious nature, requiring their attention, thought and experiment, and should more truly be termed work, even though it may have no economic value. It is during this so-called play that children learn to work, to concentrate and to persevere until achievement is reached; [4] to discover the nature of their surroundings and of the people in their community, to acquire skills of body and mind, and to express their thoughts and feelings in a great variety of ways [5].

In this description of play, the following theories are drawn upon (several of them mutually exclusive):

1 Recreation
2 Surplus energy
3 Pleasure theory
4 Preparation for life
5 Play as an integrating mechanism

What a mess we are bound to say! However, the dismissing of play in education by the work-versus-play supporters, and the overclaiming for it by the child-centred educators in the late 1960s, led to philosophers like Dearden and Peters subjecting 'play' to scrutiny and finding it muddled – what Dearden (1968, p. 94) calls: 'A still continuing child-centred tradition of eulogising play'.

Recent research and theory (1970s and 1980s)

The unease raised by philosophers of education, typified by Dearden in the 1960s, about the value of play situations pervades much of the research literature of the 1970s and 1980s. It led to a critical examination of the generic concept of play, which sought out those elements which were educationally most useful.

Within the 'play as education' group of theories, which form the bulk of theories we have looked at so far, there emerged two definite strands. The first, typified by Bruner and the Oxford Studies, the Hutts and the Tizards, supports the view that play is education, because it prepares children for future life. Play initiates children into what they will need to do in the future, in ways which are developmentally appropriate. This approach leads to the need for adults to structure play situations, and to guide play. It focuses on where play leads children for the future.

The second strand also sees play as education. It is typified by the work of Fein, Garvey, Göncü, Millar, the Singers and Tamburrini. Play is seen as an integrating mechanism which enables children to sort out their ideas, feelings and relationships; to know themselves, and to come to terms with their knowledge, understanding and experience. Through play, children master, control, innovate, create, imagine and demonstrate their uniqueness. Adults do not dominate this approach to play, but they are crucial and sensitive catalysts in its development.

These two strands of thinking both value play deeply, but adults take different roles in supporting it. In the first approach (preparing for life), we see the emphasis on directly structured, guided play led by adults. In the second, play is an integrating mechanism approach; we see an emphasis on free-flow play, with adults indirectly structuring and extending. Sometimes the child leads; sometimes the adult leads. During sustained free-flow play, adult and child are in synchrony, as in a conversation.

In the following sections we explore both strands.

Strand One – Play as preparation for life

Researchers working in the 1970s, such as Corinne and John Hutt, emphasised that in epistemic play, children learn; whilst in ludic play, they do not. In epistemic play, children explore and discover, e.g. with sand. Ludic play is imaginative play. The Oxford Studies (1980s), directed by Bruner, also emphasised play containing cognitive challenge, as superior to so-called unstructured play situations, which are not challenging. Tizard and Harvey, in the 1970s, criticised the encouragement of too much free play, again suggesting that children were not learning when involved in this. There is a suggestion that free play has no structure. As Joan Tamburrini (1982) points out, every kind of play has some kind of structure. In other words, symbolic free play is only seen to be useful where it helps later games (such as tennis) and prepares children for life. Peter Smith (1986, p. 11) points out:

> So far as free play is concerned, the possibility must be faced that it may not be as essential for cognitive growth as some previous writers have suggested.

It is this situation that has led to an emphasis by some on trying to prove that play helps children to learn. Encouraging adults to lead, structure and guide play is thought to be the answer. However, in a survey of play literature in 1983, Rubin, Fein and Vandenburg (in Smith, p. 41) distinguish play through six criteria:

1   It is intrinsically motivated.

2   It is characterised by attention to means, rather than ends.

3   It is distinguished from exploratory behaviour.

4   It involves 'as if', or pretend, behaviour.

5   There are no externally applied rules (cf games).

6   The child is not day-dreaming, but actively engaged.

The more of these criteria that are present, the more certain it is that the child is playing. This suggests that adult-led, structured or guided play is not 'play' in the sense of 'free-flow' play. In this book, we are concerned to see the value of the kind of free-flow play Rubin, Fein and Vandenburg identified through their criteria. This means we should not overclaim for play, or try to suggest it is almost the only way that children learn. As we are beginning to see, that is not what free-flow play is about. Free-flow play is concerned with the way children integrate, use and apply their knowledge and understanding. It involves reflection or metacognition, decentration, relationships and feelings, as well as physical competence and ideas. It means being an original thinker: imaginative and innovative.

Strand Two – Play as an integrating mechanism

There is a considerable body of research emphasising the importance of free-flow play in its own right – primarily as an integrating mechanism. Most of this research also recognises the importance of the child's growing awareness of, and competence in, rule formats and external scripts. It sees these as developing in synchrony with free-flow play. Such research has been influenced by child-centred theories of play, which emphasise that the child is in control when playing.

Group play, using the BillyGoat Gruff *story as a starting point for getting together.*

Catherine Garvey, at a conference on play in 1977 (Smith and Smith, p. 276), makes a strong statement for free-flow play, giving it status alongside 'games', which are not pure play, and a separate process from it. 'By looking at play only for what it might do, for what it might be good for (preparation for life), for its contextual correlates, we may miss a great deal that we could find by looking at it more closely'. She added (p. 211) 'It seems that children themselves may recognise the ability to make believe fluently as a highly valued capability'.

Vivian Gussin Paley's classroom observations of children aged three to five years bring meaning to this statement (1985, p. 81). She says of Wally (five years):

> He is not a captive of his illusions and fantasies, but can choose them for support or stimulation without self consciousness. He has become aware of the thinking required by the adult world, but is not committed to its burden of rigid consistency.

Catherine Garvey (1977, p. 32) suggests that play seems to be associated with the potentiality for adapting to changing circumstances. In her view, only lower species have a set script to which they adhere. In free-flow play, children make their own scripts, both alone and with others. As Garvey argues, free-flow play 'is an experimental dialogue with the environment', which includes materials, times, places and people.

A sample from the many research studies emphasising the importance of free-flow play in early education can be found in the Froebel Nursery Project 1972–7, directed by Chris Athey (1990); and the Froebel Block Play Collaborative Research Project, 1986–9, directed by Bruce (ed. Gura, in press, 1992). Göncü (1987) and Fein (1979) are discussed in Chapter 4.

Joan Tamburrini (1982) stresses the power of the indirectly structured curriculum, which is sufficiently open-ended for adults to act as catalysts for free-flow play. She reasserts that free-flow play is without an end-product, and that it is voluntary on the part of the child. The tradition of the early childhood curriculum, based on the principles which form its bedrock, cater for these aspects, and in so doing, value free-flow play. In her view, adults need to provide an appropriate and exciting environment, and to converse with children in ways that are sensitive to their ideas and feelings, and which look ahead to what is needed next in planning provision.

Ways Forward

Free-flow play remains a priority in early childhood education and care settings. As Peter Smith writes (1986, p. 13) 'Research should only enhance, and not detract from, this very rewarding and fascinating activity'.

There are two ways forward in emphasising the value of free-flow play. The first arises from new theory, which offers better theoretical support. Chaos theory, as it is known, is discussed in a later chapter. It offers strong and recent theoretical support for free-flow play, illuminating and enhancing its value. A second way forward can be found by examining 12 features of free-flow play.

In this chapter, the difficulties of defining play have emerged. In Chapter 4, its features are identified so that we can see when children are free-flow playing, and when they are involved in other processes. Using the 12 features of free-flow play, we can arrive at some sort of definition. We can say that free-flow play seems to be concerned with the ability and opportunity to wallow in ideas, experiences, feelings and relationships. It is also about the way children come to use the competencies they have developed. It is the way children integrate all their learning, and can be summarised in the following equation.

$$\text{Free-flow play} \quad = \quad \text{wallow} \quad + \quad \text{competence}$$

Summary

This last chapter has looked at the views and influence, primarily of researchers and theorists, in relation to the umbrella term of play (i.e. broadly defined). In the next, we look at important influences on the finer-focused area of free-flow play.

3 Important Influences on the Development of Free-flow Play

In Chapter 2, we saw that theory and research have all played a part in influencing the way we see play. This chapter takes on the finer focus of free-flow play, or play as an integrating mechanism, and looks at how its practical exemplification has been influenced by leading educationalists and others who have influenced practice.

Pioneers of free-flow play

Regarding free-flow play as the means by which children integrate and apply their learning has always had strong advocates. However, this approach to play as central to education has not been without its opponents. In the eighteenth century, Froebel's schools were closed in Prussia, and his curriculum was banned. Margaret Mc-Millan's nursery school was only saved from financial collapse by a cheque from Queen Mary in 1919 (Bradburn, 1990, p. 188). In the 1930s, Susan Isaacs was regarded as running a very wild establishment at the Malting House School, which, it was often suggested, normal children did not attend.

These pioneers of free-flow play did not regard it as relief from work, or as preparation for life, but as the integration of the child's learning. In early childhood education there has always been a band of people devoted to play viewed in this way, who have made determined and unrelenting efforts, at times in the face of great opposition, to keep free-flow play on the agenda. These people have ensured its central place in the education of the young child.

Many of these modern stalwart workers are unknown to the public, but some names from the past stand out. Whether known or not, they may be described as Penelope Lively suggests in her novel *Moontiger* (1987, p. 21):

> History is of course crammed with people who are just sitting it out. It is the front liners who are the exception – those who find themselves thus placed whether they like it or not, and those who seek involvement.

However, it is not enough to look back on the approach of the earlier pioneers of free-flow play. Being a 'front liner', and seeing free-flow play as important because it views play as the integration and application of learning, is as important now as it has ever been.

This chapter begins by looking at the ideas of Froebel (1782–1852), McMillan (1860–1931) and Isaacs (1885–1948), all of whom were pioneer educators, combining theory with practice, running schools and training teachers in the schools, and, perhaps most important, involving parents in education in general and in play in particular. Montessori, who also did this, is not considered in this book, since she thought it an insult to children to suggest they should play, and so did not develop theories in relation to it (Kilpatrick, 1914, p. 42):

> If I were persuaded that children need to play, I would provide the proper apparatus, but I am not so persuaded.

Froebel's view of play (1782–1852)

When many people hear the name 'Froebel', they automatically think 'play'. As Audrey Curtis (1986, p. 6) points out, he used the 'timeless playthings of childhood' in his curriculum. 'Balls, boards, sand, clay, for example, have made up children's play activities throughout the ages'. Froebel did not believe that a child's play is trivial, for it demonstrates personality, thinking and feeling.

David Cohen (1987) suggests that Froebel was the first educator to 'use' children's play, and, in a sense, to invade it for utilitarian purposes. He rejected the view that the function of play is preparation for adult life. Although his gifts, occupations and mother songs were pre-structured activities (Bruce, 1987), Froebel, and those teachers who worked closely with him (Barop and Langethal), began to realise that this led to a rigid, preconceived approach by adults towards the materials and activities they were using with children (Liebschner, 1985; Bruce, in Gura ed., 1992, in press). He moved towards a more open-ended approach to play. 'Froebel's play theory is not merely a didactic model but one which includes the concept of learning through each other' (Liebschner, 1985, p. 41).

The role of the adult is crucial in Froebel's approach to play. It was not, as Cohen implies, about using the child's play in order that the child should learn particular things, for that would be to advocate play as preparation for life. 'A teacher who participated in children's activities, talked to them and with them and who cared for their inner (mental, spiritual, emotional life) would soon be recognised by the child as a person to be trusted' (Liebschner, 1985). The teachers, Barop and Langethal, who worked with Froebel were skilled at helping parents to play in this way so that children learnt *through* them, not *from* them. As Gordon Wells (1987, p. 222) writes (in a modern-day context): 'The responsibility is clear, to interact with those in our care in such a way as to foster and enrich their meaning making'. This is the purpose of education. Froebel valued play because it helped children to make meaning, and, as Janet Moyles (1989, p. 168) points out, all this requires 'that adults enjoy and value playing with children'. She points out the importance of adults and children being 'equal partners in play, as in conversation'.

An example of Froebel's approach to play is given by Liebschner (1985, p. 38):

> Barop (one of Froebel's teachers) had given, in the presence of the parents, a five year old boy and a three year old girl four balls. The boy picked up the green and red, the girl the yellow and blue. After a while, the children rolled them both together on the table. The mother commented that it looked like the movement of the earth. Then they lifted them and turned them on their own axis round each other and around the hand. The mother realised that this echoed the movement of the earth. Barop notes, 'mother and father were delighted at their child's play. The children now asked their parents often whether they would join them in their play with the balls'.

Froebel believed play to be a unifying mechanism which integrates the child's learning. He saw play as the highest phase in the child's functioning, and, for this reason, considered it to be a spiritual activity. In his theory of unity, Froebel saw the child's play as the way that the universe appeared on a smaller scale, e.g. through his/her gifts and their relationship with the universe, the occupations, mother songs, garden, and through relationships in sharing them. Carolyn Steedman (1990) argues that these are metaphors.

Froebel believed play to be voluntary (e.g. as in the children and adults playing with the coloured balls). He believed that free-flow play took children beyond ordinary functioning to an intuitive sense of higher things (implicit links with the movement of the planets in the example with Barop). The relationships developed through play are central to Froebel's philosophy (Liebschner, 1985, p. 38): 'Mothers know that the first smile marks an epoch in the child's development, for it comes not from a self feeling only, but from a social feeling also'.

Froebel did not believe that children should be put under pressure to develop particular things in their play, as shown when Barop allowed the children to use the coloured balls as they wanted, and to suit their own inner purposes. Relationships were sensitive each to the other, around a firsthand experience which it was hoped would engage the children's interest. The children used their widest knowledge and physical skill, and so could try out different ideas in a reflective manner. The adult acted as a catalyst. This brought about the deep satisfaction of play and helped the children towards unity of self, unity with others, and unity with knowledge itself.

A good curriculum is a good curriculum for all

Janet Moyles (1989, p. 24) points out that Froebel pioneered the theory of firsthand experience as the basis of play. However, it is important to note that his approach was entirely different from that of Seguin (1812–1880), who developed learning through the senses as a programme for physically disabled children. Seguin emphasised (Steedman, 1990) a pre-structured programme, developing, in particular, manual dexterity, which he saw as important for the future lives of the children of manual workers. This curriculum was geared towards a particular direction, and signalled the beginnings of a 'sheep and goats' approach, which greatly influenced the curriculum. This came to a head in the late 1960s, when 'under-privileged children' were thought to require a different curriculum from the 'privileged'. Froebel's approach to play was more accessible to all children's needs than that of Seguin, who, in effect, pioneered the disadvantaged child syndrome. After all, as Yvonne Conolly (1983) points out (OMEP), 'A good curriculum is a good curriculum for all' (in Bruce, 1987, Ch. 9).

Margaret McMillan's development towards free-flow play (1860–1931)

Margaret McMillan was caught between two approaches. The first was the sense training and physical approach to education through the curriculum of Seguin, which excluded play in any sense of the word. The second was the Froebelian view: that firsthand experience, emphasising relationships, feelings and ideas as much as the physical aspects, is important, and that these experiences become integrated and applied through play. The child moves onto a higher plane of functioning through free-flow play.

Unwittingly, McMillan put herself into a conflict situation not unlike the conflict Froebel had experienced before her, and which also had to be resolved by Susan Isaacs at a later date. Perhaps it has to be resolved by anyone working directly with young children. Just as Froebel had initially used two opposing approaches at the same time – which led to an inevitable lack of logical coherence in his work – so did McMillan, and, later, so did Susan Isaacs. In Bradford, at the turn of the century, Margaret McMillan used mainly Seguin's work excluding play. (She was annoyed years later to find Montessori receiving acclaim for introducing his ideas to Britain: 'The new education is not new. It was developed in Bradford 15 years ago' – Bradburn, 1990, p. 186.) However, in 1903, she became a member of the Froebel Society. During this period, she used Seguin's sense training approach, and at the same time developed Froebel's notion of free-flow play and the garden, both in the same curriculum. These theories do not easily sit side by side.

We can see the conflict Bradburn (1990, p. 177):

Suppose you want to develop the touch sense! Lo! Here are a score of leaves, hairy sunflower, crinkled primrose, glossy fuchsia, and the rose. Do you want to compare colours, to note hues and shades? Well, here is wealth a plenty. The herb garden will offer more scents than anyone can put into a box, and a very little thought will make of every pathway a riot of opportunities.

The 'riot of opportunities', and the real flowers rather than apparatus, is more Froebelian in influence, whilst the 'you want to develop the touch sense' is the programmed approach of Seguin. In the garden, she encouraged free-flow play.

Like Susan Isaacs, McMillan could translate current theory and thinking into simple, everyday language, so that deep ideas could be proposed and shared. Also like Susan Isaacs, she could interpret and tune into the mood of the times, implicitly recognising the understandable anxieties and cautiousness of teachers, but managing to articulate what their idealistic selves wanted for young children. By not outrightly rejecting the more rigid aspects of education, she was able to encourage the desire to move further towards an idealistic approach so that people felt ownership of it, rather than threatened by it. In this way, McMillan helped teachers to understand and value free-flow play, and to strive for it.

Bradburn (1990, p. 66) points out that Margaret McMillan was operating in the Edwardian era, when the Victorian Empire was coming under threat. 'The Edwardian Age was to be marked by a sometimes feverish search for greater efficiency'. When we are insecure, we tend to tighten up and become more rigid, and this is reflected in changes to the curriculum. The way in which Margaret McMillan took up Seguin's didactic approach demonstrates her implicit tuning in to the Edwardian need for security, through tangible elements in the curriculum. On the other hand, her use of Froebel's ideas reflects her vision of a new world, in which free-flow play would contribute a major part. Brockway (1894) described her (in Bradburn, 1990, p. 46) as 'almost the perfect harmony of idealist and practical reformer'.

However, as Steedman points out, McMillan's practical side was initially out of keilter with her ideals, in that aspects of her curriculum were based on a curriculum that regarded the child as in need of remediation, i.e. a deficit model of the child. McMillan's idealistic self did not view the working-class child as deficient and in need of remediation. Through examining the thinking of Froebel, McMillan and Isaacs, we see the need for ideals in developing practice, and for principles to guide us. The curriculum that is offered needs to interweave coherently and logically, so that our ideals and our practice move forward together in promoting free-flow play.

Free-flow play in the garden of the Deptford School

The Froebelian training helped Margaret McMillan to see the child as a unified whole, with play as the integrating mechanism. It was through the garden that we see her begin to develop the free-flow play side of the curriculum, which led to greater cohesion between her ideals and the practical translation of the curriculum she offered. It is interesting to note that for Froebel, McMillan and Isaacs, it was the child's free play in the garden (the outdoors) which led to their greatest contributions to the early childhood educational curriculum.

The British nursery school, with its indoor and outdoor areas, has kept alive free-flow approaches to play in a way that is emulated throughout the world. It is one of Margaret McMillan's greatest contributions to early years education that she developed free-flow play in his way. Like Froebel, McMillan believed that the school should be the heart of the community. Like Froebel, she wanted parents to share their children's play, using the garden to do so.

Adult and children: first-hand experiences in the garden.

The garden led children to a sense of unity as they played. In the garden, free-flow play was encouraged, rather than Seguin's pre-structured sense training, using didactic apparatus. The emphasis was on the whole child; children ate, slept and played in the garden. It was a holistic and whole-making experience. 'Children experienced fresh air, trees, terraces, rock gardens, herbs, vegetables, fruit trees, bushes, opportunities to climb on walls, sand pits, lawns, flowers in flower beds, and wilderness' (Steedman, 1990).

Like any good thinker, Margaret McMillan's ideas developed, so that by 1930 – the year before her death – she was writing (*The Nursery School*, Dent, p. 80): 'Most of the best opportunities for achievement lie in the domain of free play, with access to varied material'.

Sharing the importance of free-flow play with parents

Just as Froebel wanted to share his understanding of play with parents, so Margaret McMillan tried to do so. (Steedman, 1990, p. 181.) The Deptford School was 'a system of education not just for the children involved but for their parents as well'. Froebel and McMillan were two great pioneers who stood up to be counted through their gradual realisation that children need free-flow play as part of their education. Bradburn (1990, p. 166) writes that McMillan, 'left you feeling that something ought to be done but that you ought to do it'.

Susan Isaacs' view of play (1885–1948)

Whereas McMillan was influenced by Seguin and Froebel, Susan Isaacs was influenced by Froebel, Dewey and psychoanalytic theory (first Freud, and then Melanie Klein). She valued free-flow play because it gave children freedom in their actions, thoughts and emotional expression. It opened up possibilities for inquiry, and it was an integrating process.

Initially, like McMillan and Froebel, she used didactic materials in her school (those of Montessori) and met the same conflicts of philosophy between her ideals and her practice that they had encountered. Over time, however, she became increasingly critical of the didactic sense training approach. She wrote a letter to one teacher saying:

Wherever you use it you show that you are not thinking of sense training in the narrow Montessorian meaning, but are thinking of it as referring to the child's active interest in the world outside himself. But why not say so? I don't believe that the child is ever interested in the development of his own senses, he is interested in things and the way they behave. He is interested in the colour of objects, the shapes and sizes, and mutual relations of objects and what he can do with them (in Smith, 1986, p. 155).

Arnold Campbell (in Gardner, p. 168) writes that, 'She was basically a liberal educationalist, but she did not antagonise the formalists'.

Isaacs saw free-flow play as the way children understood experiences in their lives (Gardener, 1969 p. 75). She believed that:

Children went further in discovery and learnt more by generous provision for play, with the support of skilled teachers, than they had done by being given instructions in groups or limited occupations on specially selected apparatus.

Like Froebel and McMillan, Susan Isaacs also stressed free-flow play as an integrating vehicle, and the importance for children of being able to move freely outdoors and indoors in their play. Of formal classrooms she said (Smith, p. 149): 'But how absurd! children don't learn in those places'. In her opinion (Smith, p. 68), 'it is stillness we have to justify, not movement'. Isaacs further stressed that play also meets the emotional needs of the child. As Smith writes (p. 151 National Froebel Foundation Bulletin 1948 obituary):

She could show us the whole child, functioning as a whole, and she has stopped us from thinking of learning as the sole business of the school, while emotion is relegated to the home or the clinic.

She gave play priority in the school, and helped to move Froebelian philosophy on from the rather stagnant and romantic view of play that had begun to develop, by bringing her psychoanalytic approach to bear on Froebelian theory. Children became real again – with tempers, at times being rude; with moods and with interest in their bodies. She stressed the need to observe what children actually do.

Like Froebel and McMillan, Isaacs believed that the

school should be an open place, and part of the community. 'As the process of living shapes them, so they understand it and shape themselves as well' (Smith, 1990, p. 208). She believed that imaginative free-flow play was of central importance in this.

The influence of psychoanalytic theory

Isaacs was greatly influenced by Melanie Klein's view that the adult could translate for the child the underlying symbolic function of his/her free-flow play, e.g. the purse symbolises a womb for babies. She believed it possible to begin analysis and so mitigate the harshness of the formation of the super ego (Smith). This contrasts with Anna Freud's view that it is necessary to wait until the oedipal phase of Freudian theory, and that until then, it is only possible to observe and understand the child better. However, Isaacs did agree with Anna Freud's view that there is a distinction between teacher and analyst, and that the teacher needs to exert a mild, firm authority which controls the child's most aggressive behaviour.

Isaacs (1968) saw the child during free-flow play as escaping into a world of imagination to avoid reality, but also as escaping from imagination into a world of reality. when anxiety or anger is great, children seek refuge in real-life situations, e.g. regular meals and a predicatable environment. Through free-flow play, children learn to cope with reality on their own terms, and to deal with fears and anxieties.

> If the child has ample opportunity for free play and bodily exercise, if this love of making and doing with his hands is met, if his intellectual interest in the world around him is encouraged by sympathy and understanding, if he is left free to make believe or to think as his implulses take him, then his advances in skill and interest are but the welcome signs of mental health and vigour. (p. 61)

Like Froebel and McMillan, Isaacs thought it of great value for children to meet other children in school – this is one of the central values of nursery education. 'The need for companionship is as great as the need for shelter and comfort'.

Sharing with parents

Susan Isaacs also spent much of her energy sharing what she learnt about play with parents – through radio broadcasting, as well as in print. She regularly wrote as 'Ursula Wise' in *Nursery World* (1919). Toys should be of 'simple variety that she can use in make-believe play or in construction of some sort, not merely the mechanical kind with which there is nothing much to be done' (in Smith, p. 252). She advised parents (*The Nursery Years*, p. 133) to 'leave the children free to use their playthings in their own way'.

The view of play they came to share

We have seen that Froebel developed from using his gifts in a very rigid way to a more flexible free-flow play approach. Margaret McMillan also moved from using didactic materials in a pre-sequenced way to a free-flow play situation. Likewise, Susan Isaacs abandoned didactic materials pre-structured by adults. She wrote:

> For play has the greatest value for the young child when it is really free and his own. (1968, p. 133)

John Dewey (1859–1952)

John Dewey was a great influence on the progress made throughout the 1930s to 1950s in considering the value of free-flow play. Susan Isaacs drew on his philosophy, which stressed development of the person, and the value of experience in its various aspects.

> Through free play, we see the interplay of all the child's powers, thoughts and physical movements embodying in a satisfying form his own images and interests.

Dewey helped teachers to find a responsible voice for play and to take it into their primary school classrooms.

Specialist teacher training colleges

Froebel, McMillan and Isaacs all recognised the importance for adults of understanding and studying free-flow play, and being trained to encourage it in children. Their influence far outlived the pioneers themselves, through the medium of training colleges run on the basis of their philosophies.

A number of small, specialist nursery/infant colleges grew up during the twentieth century, most of which were closed or merged with other colleges during the 1970s. These included Margaret McMillan College in Bradford, Rachel McMillan College in Deptford, Maria Grey College in Twickenham, Froebel Educational Institute in Roehampton, and the Department of Child Development, established by Susan Isaacs, at the University of London. The dedicated work of tutors in helping teachers to understand and encourage free-flow play in educational settings had a great influence, and resulted in students from these colleges being in great demand by schools, through the obvious excellence of their informed and reflective practice. Such colleges were able to focus on the educational needs of the youngest children.

The Plowden Report (1967)

The steady work that had been going on in supporting, encouraging and informing practice in relation to free-flow play was given official recognition with the Plowden Report (DES, 1967). This report has been welcomed, attacked, dissected and analysed ever since, but its major contribution was that it officially gave play a central status in the education of young children, and so it still remains. As we have seen during the 1970s and 1980s, there were influences which suggested the need to guide play, so that it became purposeful, prepared children for life, and made sure they were 'learning whilst they played'. However, we need to return to the two strands which emerged in Chapter 2, both of which see play as educational. The first leads to adult domination of children's play through guiding it. The emphasis is on play as preparation for future life. The second regards free-flow play as the integration and application of learning. Huda Nashif (1985) points out that these 'approaches have often taken extreme positions over what seemed, on the surface, to be a controversy about procedures, when the issue is fundamentally that of the perceived function of the pre-school'. A focus on preparation for adult life structures play so that it is adult dominated and adult led. A focus on the integration and application of learning can now be argued to serve the child's future adult needs better in the long term. This is expressed in Principle 1 in the first chapter:

Childhood is seen as valid in itself, as a part of life and not simply as preparation for adulthood. Thus education is seen similarly as something of the present and not just preparation and training for later.

The Plowden Report made this principal official policy, because by valuing free-flow play, it did not perceive the function of early education to be simply a preparation for life. Free-flow play was seen to be about what is appropriate for children now, and in that way it would be a catalyst for their future lives. In applying and using ideas, feelings and social interactions now, the future is also catered for.

The Early Years Curriculum Group (1988)

This reassertion of basic principles has recently been taken up with the formation of the EYCG, a group which was convened by Vicky Hurst of Goldsmiths College, London, and includes specialists and experts working in a variety of settings. It was a major influence in reasserting the importance of free-flow play at the time of the introduction of the National Curriculum in Great Britain. Rosemary Peacocke (1989, p. iv), formerly HMI Staff Inspector with responsibility for Early Years says in the Introduction that play and firsthand experience are emphasised and that 'this book places these two vital elements firmly within the context of the National Curriculum'.

Summary

In Chapter 2, we saw how theory and research help us to make a map of play (broadly defined) and the way it has been viewed. In this chapter, we have seen some common strands between past and present approaches to free-flow play. A central issue is the extent to which adults should lead play. If the main function of play is seen as preparing children for adult life, then adults need to structure and guide play.

If play is seen primarily as an integrating mechanism, adults need to be trained to appreciate, understand and support children's control of it; and to extend it sensitively, seeing it as the method by which children make sense of their learning, and apply it (Tamburrini, 1981). This approach also prepares children for adult life – it both integrates the child's learning now, and prepares for the future. Parents should be informed about free-flow play, as well as other approaches to play, so that their children do not miss out on a central part of their education.

4 Free-flow Play and its Features

The state of play

We have seen in Chapter 1 how the three Cs influence the curriculum. The child, the context and the content are all crucial elements. In Chapter 2, we looked at different theories of play and the way these influence practioners and researches in their approach to free-flow play. We began to see that 'play' is a word that has different meanings for different people. That is why, when we use the word, we need to use adjectives that signal our meaning to others. In this book, the adjectives used to describe play are 'free-flow'.

In the next two chapters, we shall see that free-flow play is part of a network of related processes in the child, which include struggle, exploration, manipulation, discovery and practice – all catalysts to the child's development. Representation, games and humour are all processes which develop alongside free-flow play, and all these processes feed off and into each other (discussed in Chapters 5 and 6).

This chapter looks at some of the crucial features which enable us to identify when a child is engaged in free-flow play. This will help us to tease out how free-flow play differs from struggle, exploration and practice, or from representation, games and humour, which are some of the processes often put under the umbrella term 'play'. Researchers such as the Hutts (1970s) have tried to ease the confusion by distinguishing between exploratory play and ludic (imaginative) play. Alternatively, we could abandon the word altogether, but then we might throw out the baby with the bathwater, so to speak. Overall, the best way forward seems to be to use adjectives to describe and signal our meaning of play when we use the word.

Free-flow play is valuable in the child's education and unique in the contribution it makes. As we saw in Chapter 2, if it is seen as recreation, it only takes place as a break from work. If it is seen to be useful, mainly in preparing children for adult life, it leads us to believe that only structured or guided play can be educational. Bruner's theory has had a great influence on researchers and schools in this respect.

If, on the other hand, we see play as important, in terms of helping children to integrate their learning and to use what they learn, to apply their knowledge in new and fascinating ways – innovatively, imaginatively, uniquely and in a manner which makes, to use Donaldson's phrase, 'human sense' of what they have learnt – we are more likely to set up educational environments where free-flow play is encouraged. The theories of Freud, Klein, Erikson, Winnicott, Piaget and Vygotsky are all in agreement here, although for Piaget and Vygotsky, there is a gradual development in early junior school towards games with externally imposed rules, rather than the personal, idiosyncratic and intrinsic rules of free-flow play. The psychodynamic theories of Freud, Klein, Erikson and Winnicott are all closed, rather than open-ended theories. This means that they are not easily open to modification and extension in the same way as the theories of Bruner, Piaget and Vygotsky. They are a whole package, which must either be accepted, or not. Since they raise gender issues, and are male dominated, they are unsatisfactory in important ways. However, they are the psychological theories which offer support for free-flow play as a system in its own right, and as one which develops throughout life.

Sometimes, however, theoretical support comes from unexpected quarters. Whoever would have thought that a topologist in the eighteenth century and a weatherman in the meteorological office in the 1960s would offer us theoretical support for the inclusion of free-flow play in education? The recent developments in Chaos Theory during the 1980s could have an important influence on the way free-flow play is valued and given status.

We shall see in the remainder of this chapter that the theory we have explored so far has led to the possiblity of formulating 12 features of free-flow play. We shall then see (Chapter 7) that the formulation of these features can also be linked with the recently developing Chaos Theory emerging from mathematics, and into a rich diversity of fields.

The 12 features of free-flow play

Rubin, Fein and Vandenburg (1983) formulated criteria of play (see Chapter 2) and these have been absorbed, where indicated, in the first four features below. However, free-flow play has other crucial features which need to be present. If all 12 features are there, we can be more confident that we are observing free-flow play than if only a few are present.

Feature 1

It is an active process without a product (Rubin *el al.*, adapted).

Feature 2

It is intrinsically motivated (Rubin *el al.*, adapted).

Feature 3

It exerts no external pressure to conform to rules, pressures, goals, tasks or definite direction (Rubin *el al.*, adapted).

Feature 4

It is about possible, alternative worlds, which involve 'supposing' (Rubin *el al.*, adapted)., and 'as if' (Atkins, 1988), which lift players to their highest levels of functioning. This involves being imaginative, creative, original and innovative.

Feature 5

It is about participants wallowing in ideas, feelings and relationships. It involves reflecting on and becoming aware of what we know, or 'metacognition'.

Feature 6

It actively uses previous firsthand experiences, including struggle, manipulation, exploration, discovery and practice (Rubin *el al.*, adapted).

Feature 7

It is sustained, and when in full flow, helps us to function in advance of what we can actually do in our real lives.

Feature 8

During free-fow play, we use the technical prowess, mastery and competence we have previously developed, and so can be in control.

Feature 9

It can be initiated by a child or an adult, but if by an adult he/she must pay particular attention to features 3, 5 and 11.

Feature 10

It can be solitary.

Feature 11

It can be in partnerships, or groups of adults and/or children who will be sensitive to each other.

Feature 12

It is an integrating mechanism, which brings together everything we learn, know, feel and understand.

If we want a shorthand way to summarise the 12 features of free-flow play, we can express their essence in an equation.

Free-flow play = wallowing in ideas, + application of
                   feelings and   developed
                   relationships   competence,
                                           mastery and
                                           control

Feature 1   Free-flow play is an active process without a product

In drawing together research on play, Moyles (1989, p. 11) states that 'play must be viewed as a process'. This process of free-flow play uses firsthand experiences of struggling, manipulating, exploring, discovering and practising, and forms a network with other processes such as games, humour and representation.

Adults often become anxious when children are thought to be purposeless or off-task. This only matters in situations where a product of some kind is necessary or required. The essence of free-flow play is that products are not necessary or desirable. Free-flow play has no set tasks, definite outcomes or products. When children play in this way, they are without pressure to complete anything, achieve anything or perform anything. That is the strength of free-flow play. For example, Hannah (six years), Anna (five years) and Emily (six years) are playing with Leo (six years) and James (six years) in the woods. It is the popular 'chase' type of free-flow play. The girls set up 'Dock Leaf hospital', and when participants are stung by nettles, they go there to have juice squeezed on the sting. The play free-flows along with no purpose or product, but a great deal of rushing about and shouting.

This contrasts with 'representation', which emphasises both process and product. Often the product will be idiosyncratic and personal, rather than public and shared. Barbara (seven years), Helen (eight years) and Penny (seven years) make a den out of an outline wall structure of sticks and pineneedles, as wattle and daub, to fill the cracks. The process of building is exciting. Once the den is completed, they leave it. It is a representation, and does not lead into free-flow play.

Sometimes children use representations in their free-flow play. Bobbie (four years) and Jo (six years) spend a morning making Zorro costumes, using dressing-up clothes and materials. After lunch, they used them to play 'Zorro'. In the process of making the costumes, a representational product results. This product is then used in the process of free-flow playing.

Because Bruner (In Roberts and Tamburrini, 1981) emphasises the importance of process and product, he focuses on representation more than free-flow play. In contrast, Vygotsky (1978, p. 101) sees play as a higher developmental processes, and gives it great status in the early years as a 'leading factor in development'.

We can see from the above examples that children move in and out from free-flow play to representation, and back again. This is almost, as John Matthews (1988) suggests, imperceptible at times.

Feature 2 Free-flow play is intrinsically motivated

A teacher of four year olds says to Sade, 'Come and play with me'. She sits on the floor with the small-world road layout, cars, houses and playpeople. Sade joins her. The teacher says, 'I want to make something to do with the visit to the shops yesterday. What do you think?'. Sade picks up a house – 'This can be the launderette' – and puts it on the road. They are off – neither is making the other do anything. They are both there because they want to be, either could leave at any time, but they don't. They make suggestions to each other, and develop the play in a way that is sensitive to each other.

This contrasts with Jake's teacher who asks him to play. She asks him where they went first, and gets him to put that shop on the road. Although Jake willingly joins in, he is responding to the teacher's ideas, rather than being encouraged to initiate his own. Throughout, the teacher controls and keeps ownership of the ideas, as she guides the direction of the reconstruction of the visit to the shops. Sade is free-flow playing with her teacher. Jake is joining a teacher-led task. Sade is intrinsically motivated through the initiatives she is able to make in free-flow playing, Jake is not.

In Bruce (1987), 10 principles forming the bedrock of the early childhood traditions were put forward. The fourth values intrinsic motivation, which leads us to value free-flow play, such as Sade's. Kellmer Pringle (1980, p. 33) stresses the importance of 'the willingness or motivation to learn and make progress'. Sade is developing this because she has a sense of owning her free-flow play in partnership with her teacher. Kellmer Pringle also emphasises that 'the essential driving force of the will to learn has its roots in the quality of relationships available to the child right at the beginning of life'. Sade's teacher is encouraging, rather than cutting across, her intrinsic motivation as they free-flow play together.

Feature 3   Free-flow play exerts no external pressure to conform to rules, pressures, goals, tasks or definite directions

In reality, children often have their own sense of direction in their play, but it is not externally imposed. In Bruce (1987, p. 80) Grace and Hannah free-flow played 'dancers'. They had their own personal rules, and each had her own idiosyncratic agenda, which was important if the play was to continue. However, they were prepared to submit themselves to the pressures of each other's ideas and to be sensitive to them, in order that their play did not collapse.

Three-year-old Gracie wears a ballet tutu, and loves to jump in it enjoying the bounce of the skirt. Her four-year-old friend, Hannah, wants her to walk round in a circle, supporting her while she balances on one leg to ballet music. Hannah is trying to re-enact the ballet 'La Fille Mal Gardee', which she has previously seen. She needs Gracie in order to relive this joy, and must keep her in the free-flow play or it will fade. Gracie is encouraged to jump at the end of each section, so that she is happy to keep playing. Both children submit themselves to rules which help them to be sensitive to each other. These are not external rules or pressures; they come from within. They are part of this play, and will fade when the free-flow play finishes.

In the same way, a group of students had no definite direction or rules to follow, but simply a shared thought to start them off in their free-flow play.

A drama group of 20 year olds were told to improvise for 20 minutes to 'warm up', as their tutor would be late. They had worked together for two years (12 students), one day a week. Someone shouted – 'Lets do Wellington Boots'. Another said, 'It sounds like an opera, I'll be leading lady'. Another said, 'We need a chorus'. Their tutor arrived and one of them pretended to give her a programme, and showed her to a seat. The chorus began to sing something in harmony. The only words sung were 'Wellington Boots', though no-one had said that was how it would be. The main parts came on and did exaggerated gestures, and sang with vigour and tragedy, etc. Everyone bowed. The tutor applauded.

Free-flow play has a rough, general script (Wellington Boots) based on real experiences (in this case, everyone had experienced Wellington Boots and opera). No-one had to do this group play, or follow its direction with other participants. This is different from the pressures of external rules. There are external rules, external pressures, and a definite direction in the following mathematics game.

A student has made a maths game. She invites three children (four years old) to join in with her. It involves throwing a cube with a picture on each side and finding the picture in a box. This picture is then placed on a model island, and after three clues, a treasure is taken from a box in the middle of the island. No-one wins. Everyone gets a treasure when they have completed their three clues.

These children are not free-flow playing; they are taking part in a maths game. This is not to suggest that the mathematics game is not valuable, but it is not free-flow play. It is, as we shall see in Chapter 6, a game with pre-set and externally set rules, and a disembedded context.

> Disembedded tasks are not spontaneous, they are set by the adult, and children must in turn 'set' their minds to them with deliberate constraint and self-control (Margaret Donaldson *et al.*, 1983, p. 4).

Feature 4   Free-flow play is about possible, alternative worlds which involve 'supposing' and 'as if' which lift players to their highest levels of functioning. This involves being imaginative, original, innovative and creative

In Chapter 6, we shall look at representation as a process inter-related with free-flow play, but also separate from it. We shall look at the difference between the directionless ideas and scripts of free-flow play, and the more definite form or product they begin to take in representation.

The following children make an 'as if' situation around a shared idea and experience of large department stores.

Wally (five years), Rachel (five years), Hannah (four years), Gracie (three years) and Tom (two years) are playing 'shops' together on a rainy day. (These children know each other well). A wardrobe has been put in a room downstairs ready to move upstairs. It is in two parts, a chest of drawers and a cupboard with hanging space. The children dress up with bags, coats, hats, etc., in the typical 'playing shops' way, announcing roles and theme as Göncü suggests. Tom goes into the cupboard, which is on the floor. Rachel maintains the theme – 'That can be the lift in the shop'. The play moves forward organically. There is not enough room for everyone. Mother suggests the lift takes Tom and Gracie first and then comes back for Hannah and Wally. Gracie and Tom fight to get in. She recognises the fact that the children will not be able to wait too long for a turn.

None of these children visits department stores often, and clearly the idea of lifts in stores is something that touches them emotionally. Different children act as catalysts to maintain the play, and it self-regulates along for nearly an hour, with 'going up', pretend touching of switches and real opening and shutting of the door. Wally then finds a toy crane and plays with that, removing himself from the play. Tom wanders off as soon as he had had enough of being in and out of the lift. Rachel and Hannah agree to terminate the play – 'Let's do something else' – and it fades.

No-one ever bought anything in the shop – the lift took over. The role of the adult had been crucial in maintaining the play in the early stages – she acted as a catalyst to the group play, which was imaginative, original, creative and innovative.

The department store play took place in a home setting. The following example took place in Bridlington Nursery School. The nursery nurse sensed that a group of three and four year olds were trying to develop an 'as if' idea, but she wasn't clear quite what it was. She held back, staying near in case it became dangerous. She noticed the children were piling large, hollow blocks carefully, so that they wedged with each other to form an uneven slope. It transpired that the children were free-flow playing 'as if' they were 'climbing the Matterhorn'. Several children had parents who enjoyed rock climbing. Again, the adult was a catalyst to this play by being sensitive to it, and by staying near to help it develop safely if the need arose.

Feature 5   Free-flow play is about participants wallowing in ideas, feelings and relationships. It involves reflecting on and becoming aware of what we know, or 'metacognition'

Tom (three years) saw a child being smacked at the bus stop. He asked why the mummy smacked. His mother replied that perhaps the mummy was tired at the end of the day.

A few days later he was taken for his vaccination at the clinic. Whilst waiting, a mother said to her child, 'If you don't cry, you can have a sweety, If you do, I'll smack you'. Tom was impressed. He cried when he saw the needle coming towards him and the doctor, with the mother's permission, gave him a sweet.

Tom tried to unravel the variety of strands. He had seen a mother who smacks for no apparent reason of naughtiness in the child (he is interested in cause and effect) and a child who will be smacked for crying during an unpleasant vaccination experience, where he is rewarded for crying. He played 'smacked children' with his china doll for several days. As Field and Reite (1984) suggest, children use play to deal with unpleasant or puzzling, as well as pleasant, experiences, and get them under control through wallowing and reflecting on events. Children become involved in metacognition, reflecting on their learning and experiences as they wallow in an idea during free-flow play. Tom kept smacking the china doll, or giving her pretend sweets, chatting all the time.

Hannah (two and a half years) spent an afternoon driving around the house in a pedal car, trying to find parking spaces. She lived in Camden Town, and her mother had great difficulty in this respect. Her mother's agitation on the previous day had affected Hannah, and this emerged in the play. Hannah had developed a rough script (Nelson and Seidmans, 1984) which was helping her to reconstruct and reinterpret events.

Susan Isaacs emphasised the function of free-flow play in helping children to wallow in ideas, feelings and relationships, and distinguished between free-flow play in education and in therapy. This book does not attempt to deal with the important part played by free-flow play in therapy. Where children have experienced traumatic situations, they may need specialist support in their free-flow play, which mainstream teachers are not trained to offer.

Fein (1981) suggests that children naturally use experiences which touch them emotionally. Morag (three years) has a new baby brother. She plays washing the baby, dressing the baby, feeding the baby. She has a bathing bikini top which she uses as her breastfeeding bra. She keeps telling the baby, 'Go to sleep, darling baby, so I can read to my little girl'. She bashes the baby doll to stop it crying. In her free-flow play, she faces, deals with, and wallows in her feelings about, and relationship with, the new baby.

Free-flow play in a partnership.

Feature 6   Free-flow play actively uses previous firsthand experiences, including struggle, manipulation, exploration, discovery and practice

Firsthand experiences, such as those involving struggle, manipulation, exploration, discovery or practice, are not free-flow play as such. However, free-flow play makes use of firsthand experiences, and indeed is impoverished if there is a scarcity of these. Firsthand experience is the bedrock: the basis of free-flow play.

Anthea (eight years), Helen (nine years), Daphne (seven years) and Marc (four and a half years) play 'space ships' in the woods. There is a space ship (in an enclosure of trees), and there is outer space – dangerous to visit. They wear tiny, homemade booklets pinned inside their sweatshirts, containing pictures of people making semaphore-like signals with flags. These are secret codes. They have a space school where a teacher teaches the codes, scratching on the ground with a stick. They pretend to eat space food of toadstools, moss, etc., on plates of leaves. They have a control panel – a log on which they place pebbles, which when touched are the controls. They sleep clinging to the walls of trees. They visit Mars, Jupiter, etc., and have adventures. They report back to Earth, using announcer/reporter type voices. Marc goes off on 'reckies', which keeps him happy. In order to walk in space, he must skip. This is taken up by the group, so that anyone leaving the spaceship has to skip, or be rescued with a skipping rope belonging to Helen.

There are elements of past experiences for each of the participants as they free-flow play. Marc has mastered the struggles of learning to skip, and having practised this in many contexts, now uses his technical prowess as part of his free-flow play. Helen has been doing an Autumn project at school and is fascinated by toadstools, having man-ipulated them and explored their properties (poisonous). She uses her knowledge, acquired from Nature classes at school, to find toadstools. Anthea is intrigued by secret codes, having seen a film with morse code used in it, and through learning semaphore at Brownies, she makes up her own code. Daphne knows you can draw on wet sand from her beach experiences, and enjoys translating this to a forest floor situation, something she discovered possible last Summer. Anthea and Marc had recently flown in a small aeroplane and saw the control panel. Marc recently saw bats in a barn, clinging to the wall. Helen visited the London Planetarium and uses her knowlege of the planets. Anthea imitates the voice and intonation of a reporter from 'John Craven's News Round' on Children's BBC TV: 'This is Anthea, BBC, Mars'.

Different experiences of individuals in the group are used to establish personal agendas, arising from firsthand experiences which have previously involved struggles, discoveries, etc. (Marc and the skipping). Shared experiences also help the group agenda to develop in an organic way as the play free-flows, e.g. eating, sleeping, and taking up

Marc's skipping agenda to travel outside the spaceship (Nelson and Seidmans, 1984). In this way, the group can be sensitive to the previous firsthand experiences of those playing, and yet develop some kind of shared agenda which allows group interaction and gives the free-flow play some sense of focus and direction. It gives those playing the maximum freedom to draw on their own individual experiences, whilst at the same time bringing the shared aspects of their experiences together in a form that allows sensitive group play to free-flow.

Feature 7 Free-flow play is sustained, and when in full flow, helps us to function in advance of what we can actually do in our real lives.

In a nursery school, Christopher (four years) says, 'I'm Elvis', and moves accordingly, whilst strumming on an old guitar. Barbara (four years) dances in style while he plays and then flops down on the floor. Other children join and pick up instruments from the music table. Some play the instruments, some dance about. Suddenly, Christopher announces, 'I'm the DJ', and does some patter – 'Hallo, ladies and gentlemen. It's really good to see you here'. The children pause from playing while he does this. Then he shouts, 'Elvis', and they all begin to play again. This free-flow play continues for about 10 minutes.

In real life, Christopher is not a DJ, nor can he play the guitar and sing to it. In free-flow play, he can.

In Bridlington Nursery School, the same group free-flow played with the large hollow blocks once more. They made a smoother slope, again demonstrating great competence in the safe placing of the blocks. As before, the nursery nurse held back, letting them actively initiate and problem solve to make a large, safe slope. A child asked the other children to stand back, and then carefully pushed a large plank down the slope. Then the children allowed one child at a time to stand on a plank and slide down the slope. The nursery nurse was intrigued. They told her it was a ski slope.

The free-flow play developed across the days for sometime, using different rough 'scripts', or personal agenda, always based on flying trajectories. It was important that the children were allowed actively to initiate, problem solve, negotiate, arrange, rearrange and wallow, with a sensitive adult as a catalyst. This meant they could move into the highest gear, and become involved in what we call 'sustained and rich play'. This is the kind of free-flow play accorded status by Vygotsky, which takes children beyond their actual functioning. The headteacher and nursery school reported that one could see at a certain stage in the free-flow play the transition from the warming up and coming together of the group to a higher phase of operating, as the free-flow got under way. None of these children can yet ski at the standard they free-flow played. Free-flow play helped them to go beyond real-life experience and become 'a head taller than themselves', as Vygotsky describes it. It is perhaps true that many adults have not experienced the highest levels of free-flow play at any point in their lives, and so find it hard to appreciate.

Feature 8   During free-flow play we use the technical prowess and competency we have previously developed, and so we can be in control

When children play, they draw on their experiences – from the basis of both shared and personal knowledge. They try out what they know; what they have been learning. They bring to bear the competencies they have been developing. Through their firsthand experiences, they have imagined, explored, practised and become competent and proficient in a variety of ways across a variety of media. In free-flow play, we see the technical prowess of children.

GPs have recently reported an increase in fathers with broken arms, since the new craze of skateboarding. Whereas their children have developed, through struggling and practising, the competence necessary to free-flow play with a skateboard (and to wallow in the use of it), most fathers have not.

We see the competence children have developed in their characterisations – the withering look, the pretending to talk to a baby, the clothes selected to represent something, the props designed. Children are often uncomfortably accurate in their portrayals, e.g. Lady Jane's dress shop run by four to eight year olds had a complaints department, and the dialogue between a complainant and shopworker sounded remarkably like a conversation that had taken place in the Gas Showroom between mother and manager a few days earlier. The use of language, tone, face, body movement, mime and props was impressive. There were account books in the shop. One of the girls had recently seen her father going through his bank statements. There was a switchboard, using ideas from the one seen at the local swimming bath/recreation centre. There was a tape compiled by the girls, with music such as is often heard in department stores. There were snacks made from sponge, painted and cut with an effect that would have impressed Andy Warhol. Each customer had a coherent character who chose clothes accordingly, and who spoke to the shop assistant in character.

Interruptions were built into the game, 'Could you hold the line please?' etc. The general script or agenda was a catalyst to the personal, and they free-flowed for long periods, resuming the play after lunch (Göncü, 1987).

Interestingly, the props had been made bit by bit, with different small groups – and this play of 'Lady Jane' continued with different children visiting the house for several weeks. The props, theme, characterisations were all central aspects, demonstrating the competence of the children involved in the play in a variety of ways. Each child contributed to it in a way that added to the general 'script', so that it changed direction according to who was playing on each day.

Feature 9 Free-flow play can be initiated by a child or an adult, but if by the adult he/she must pay particular attention to Features 3, 5 and 11

Hannah draws Tom into free-flow play, as together they wallow in the idea of St George and the Dragon.

Hannah (six years) and Tom (three and a half years) play using a rough 'script', or agenda, around the idea of St George and the Dragon. Hannah says, 'Let's play George and the Dragon'. This is a general statement, so that they both have an idea with a rough sense of direction (Nelson and Seidmans 1984). Hannah says, 'I'll be the dragon'. She begins to roar. She announces her identity, using sound props, and moves into role. As Bateson writes, she is signalling, 'This is play'. Tom is new to this kind of play, he needs a prop and goes off to fetch his sword. While he is gone, Hannah screams. When he returns, she says, 'I'd rather be the maiden in distress'. 'But I haven't got anything to kill' (Tom). He puts cushions in the middle of the floor. He stabs while she screams, giving exaggerated gestures of distress. He enjoys stabbing for some time, and she enjoys screaming. She then puts on music and their movements continue for the duration of the record. She says, 'I don't want to do this any more. Mum, can we have a drink?'.

Hannah is initiating Tom into what is involved in sustained free-flow pretend play, and helping him towards being able to take part in a large group play. After the general statement that they will play George and the Dragon, which gives them a shared context, they both need to negotiate their personal agenda. Hannah announces hers, and moves into role non-verbally. She uses movement and facial expression. It takes him effort to get his role organised, but he picks up the non-verbal cues and gets himself the prop he needs (his sword). She re-negotiates her personal agenda by changing roles, but not with the general statement. She helps him to maintain his personal agenda by finding him a substitute dragon to kill (probably implicitly realising that he is too young and inexperienced in pretend play to cope with having his personal agenda changed). They reach the point of free-flow play. It begins to fade, so Hannah maintains it by putting on appropriate music. She terminates the game, leaving the story without direction, and clearly signalling that she is doing so. The play lasted for half an hour.

There is often debate about whether it is a feature of play that the child must always initiate it. Vygotsky (1978, p. 102) is useful here. He puts forward the notion of a zone of potential development. This means that (p. 87), 'What a child can do with assistance today she will be able to do by herself tomorrow'.

In fact, adults or children can initiate play, and younger children are often drawn in first as spectators, and then followers of the play – as Tom was in the free-flow play with Hannah. This is why it is desirable to have three and four year olds together in nurseries. Three year olds can often free-flow play with an older child, but not initiate it. Peter Smith (in Roberts and Tamburrini, 1981) stresses the importance of children following, leading and negotiating. In a previous example, the adult helped the younger children in the 'shop lift' play to keep playing. Both adults and children can help each other into free-flow play.

The teacher in Redford House Nursery noticed that the home corner was in a mess, and that no-one was in there. She went in, and Kelly (three years) and Anna (three years) saw her there. Kelly asked, 'What are you doing?'. The teacher replied, 'I've just got in from work, and there's been a burglary in my house. The burglars have thrown everything on the floor. I'm waiting for the police to come and see. Are you the police?' Kelly and Anna rushed around the room shouting, 'Nee Naw Nee Naw', and zoomed into the house. 'We are the police', they announced. They began to exert control over the way the story developed, playing in a typical 'follow-my-leader' manner. They chased imaginary robbers, but the thrill was the chasing rather than the catching. They kept returning to the house for cups of tea, to report on not catching the robbers. The teacher stayed there, cleaning up a little, but mainly attracting other children to play by her very presence in the home corner.

The role of the adult as a catalyst for free-flow play is central. It does not just happen. When adults initiate play, as in the above example, it is essential that they bear in mind particularly Features 3, 5 and 11.

It is important to remember that Sade was helped to free-flow play, whilst Jake was led into an adult-dominated task. The challenge for adults lies in not giving tasks, or guiding play, so that it begins to conform to the adults' ideas, leaving the children's contribution as secondary. When people come together and free-flow play, all participants need to wallow in ideas, feelings and relationships. Adults have a tendency to believe that the ideas they are currently wallowing in are the most important ones (e.g. attainment targets in the National Curriculum, or a project on 'myself', or 'this week's number is four', so the home corner has four of everything in it). We need to remind ourselves, as adults, that if we are to be good, valued and successful participants in free-flow play, we must be sensitive to the children. This last point is taken up in Feature 11.

Feature 10   Free-flow play can be solitary

Children do not have to be alone in order to play alone. For example, Kate (four years) kept her dolls house next to the draining board. While her mother performed household tasks, she would often sit on the draining board and play with the dolls house, making up stories which seemed to grow as she free-flow played.

Anthea (seven years) attended church whilst staying with a friend. This was a new experience for her. When she returned home, she made a church in her bedroom. She made an altar, with vases of flowers (daisies, dandelions, etc.) and a cross. She used a frilly skirt to create an altar cloth. She put her dolls and soft toys in rows, as in pews. She collected lavender from the garden and rubbed the flowers into a colander. She put a match to the lavender, which made incense-like smoke, and swung it on a string, dressed in her nightdress and a cape, singing in cantational tones. She picked out the tune 'All Things Bright and Beautiful' on a toy xylophone (the organ), and said 'Amen'.

Solitary free-flow play is important.

Solitary play does not mean that children are lonely. Nor does it means that children are isolated. Some experiences are best free-flow played alone. Adults, as well as children, often opt to be alone, even in a crowd.

We need to be aware of when children wish/need to engage in solitary play, so that others do not take the props they need. We also need to keep an eye on solitary play, to check it is safe (e.g. Anthea and the matches). It is significant, perhaps, that she was at home.

Children may need help in developing access strategies into partner or group play. These were discussed in Bruce (1987, pp. 129–30).

Feature 11   Free-flow play can be in partnerships, or groups of adults and/or children, who will be sensitive to each other

Play partnerships

There are certain things that have to happen before play partnerships can be successful. Hartup (1983) observed in the parallel play of young children that they developed co-ordinated gestures. For example, Siobhan (15 months) watches Amanda (15 months), who is sucking a plastic doll's head. Amanda throws it down. Siobhan throws down the car she holds. Amanda seems to notice and picks up a car. Siobhan picks up a plastic box. Amanda throws the car down. Siobhan does the same with the box. These movements are helping the children towards partner play, with a general agenda or script.

Evie (three years) has both partial sight and partial hearing. After lunch, the younger children sleep. Evie doesn't but is involved in quiet activities. She sits down at a table with jigsaws. Dominic (five years) who has partial hearing and is physically disabled, notices this. She comes to the table. Evie stands up. They synchronise sitting and bobbing up and down together and begin to shriek with laughter. The adult stops the play, because of the sleepers.

Amandip (three years), whose first language is Punjabi, was pretending to write a letter, using his own personal writing. Jenny (three years) came into the home corner and went to the dressing-up clothes. She put on a cloak and hat. 'I'm going shopping,' she announces. 'Shall I post your letter?' He replies, 'It's India'. She says, 'Here's your stamp' and hands him a stamp.

In this exchange, as Göncü (1987) suggests, each child announces their identity. It is implicitly as if Jenny says, 'I am Mummy. Who are you?', and he implicitly replies, 'I'm writing a letter to India'. Studies have also found that young children usually move straight into role without prior discussion. It is as if the non-verbal messages that they want to play together are the important ones. In effect, Bateson (1955) suggests this gives the message, 'This is play'. Jenny's facial expression signals play; so does the tone of her voice, and the way she moves in her costume.

Children need solo play to help them to develop their narratives, 'scripts', in the way they want, and to have some control and ownership of their own agenda of play. They also learn how to play with others in a manageable way, playing in parallel and cooperatively with a partner adult or child. Solitary and group play develops in synchrony.

Jason (three years) is profoundly deaf. He is at an adventure playground. Billy (four years) is partially sighted. He has a push-along truck. He is aware of another person's presence and calls out, 'Get in and I'll push you'. Jason doesn't hear. The adult explains to Billy, that Jason can't hear. He asks to be led to Jason. Jason sees him approaching with an adult and shrugs. Billy doesn't know he shrugs. Finally, Billy takes hold of Jason's hand and together they go to the truck and play together. How did they know the plan?

What Göncü (1987) calls 'free-flow pretend play' is probably the kind of play Froebel referred to as 'the highest phase' in a child's learning, or the kind of play that Vygotsky saw as making a child a 'head taller' than he/she really is. Typically, it comes to fruition betwen four and eight years. It is possible that many children never experience this level of free-flow pretend play as a group, either at home or in school. It requires both opportunities, and adults prepared to act as catalysts. It needs time to develop, rich resources, space and children experienced enough and competent enough to wallow in the play and be competent in it.

Young children have a tendency just to launch into play (as Jenny and Amandip did), both using their own personal agenda/script. If these agendas clash, the play stops – because there is no shared context. No wonder sustained free-flow play is hard for children just entering nursery education.

From partnerships to group play

Typically, children from three to five years begin to make general statements, as well as announcing their own personal agenda, but still cannot easily resolve conflicts of interest with someone else's agenda, as we saw in the example of Grace and Hannah. According to Gearhart, most children at six years old begin to share play plans, and to resolve difficulties. (In Göncü 1987)

In the main, from three to five years old, children are learning how to reach the point of free-flow play in a group – although we know that children vary tremendously in the ages at which they do things. Nevertheless, it is a tragedy and a waste if they do not have opportunities to develop into this kind of high-level functioning.

Groups who know each other

In Bruce (1987, p. 143), the example is given of a group of children playing King Arthur. Nelson and Seidmans (1984) suggest that when playing as a group, older children first negotiate an advance script or general statement. The younger children in this group (four and five years) found themselves in the play of King Arthur without perhaps knowing very much about it. (As we saw from the earlier examples of younger children, they tend to just announce their role, and begin to play.) Matthew (five years) and Kit (four years) zoomed into their personal agendas, and began to pretend gallop and wield sticks as swords, wearing cloaks. However, Hannah (seven years) expected them to play according to the general statement. She realised something was wrong, and asked, 'Do you know the story?'. They didn't and so Robin Hood was agreed upon. Matthew was experienced and old enough to sustain this and, adjusting his personal agenda, he switched to an imaginary bow and arrow – as did Tom (five years). Kit, the youngest, retained his personal agenda. He had enjoyed the cloak and stabbing the ground with a stick and continued. Sometimes he was left to do this. Sometimes Hannah alerted him to the need to conform more. In this way, he was able to remain in the play. As we have seen, older children often help younger children into group play. Kit experienced free-flow play, but he needed help in being sensitive to others free-flowing in relation to him.

The free-flow of the Robin Hood play faded when Tom found a Cardinal beetle in a bush and called everyone to look. The play had no goal, no task to complete, so this was fine.

Adults playing

An Open University programme on drama showed a group of actors improvising around a Shakespearian text. In the discussion after, they pointed out that they were used to being together and so could quickly establish non-verbal signals, as they developed their roles and improvised in getting to know the script together. Here, there is a moving towards a definite script, although the means of reaching it is free-flow play, which develops in more organic ways.

Children who often play together do the same. It is difficult to free-flow play in a group, and when children or adults become involved in it, they can sustain the play more easily if they know each other well. They have some understanding of how each person thinks, feels and approaches things, which they can prepare for and take account of as they move forward in the play. We saw this in the aquarian play of the dragon fish, and the Wellington Boots opera.

In Bruce (1987, p. 137), three guidelines are described, which help us to encourage children to be sensitive to others. These are: experiencing sensitivity by adults towards themselves; adults helping children to make meaning of their learning; and recognising that the most powerful strategy for doing so is to encourage free-flow play.

Feature 12   Free-flow play is an integrating mechanism, which brings together everything we learn, know, feel and understand

Free-flow play is about the way we apply and use what we have experienced and know as it becomes integrated and whole. It is the way children make sense of their learning education. It shows us the learning that has occurred, and how it is being taken up, dealt with and developed by the child. Through free-flow play, children can gain control over their lives, and over their knowledge and understanding, and feelings and relationships with others. In this book, we have seen that theories giving free-flow play a central place in early childhood education are predominant. Some have a cognitive emphasis (e.g. Bruner, Hutt, Tizard) and stress the products, or outcomes, of play, as it prepares children for future life.

Other theories emphasise free-flow play as an integrating mechanism, and suggest that free-flow play is unique in its contribution to development. Through emphasising its process, outcomes or products are also, in the long term, enriched (e.g. Piaget, Vygotsky, Garvey, Erikson, Winnicott, Singer, Isaacs, Tamburrini, Rubin, Fein, Vandenburg, Athey, Millar). Garvey summarises this by saying that free-flow play 'is an experimental dialogue with the environment', which includes people, materials, times, events, places and culture. For example, Anne (five years) is playing 'schools' in the garden. There is a clump of snapdragons. She pretends these are the children in the class and that she is the teacher. She pretends it is lunchtime and tips water into each one, pulling the flowerhead apart to do so. She chats in teacher tones, 'Good boy – what a nice clean plate' etc.

We see a process – with no definite line of direction – voluntarily undertaken, alone. It makes use of two real experiences – first, of recently starting at school, and second, of having lunch with a friend where mother is very keen on clean plates at the end of a meal. It is sustained, and moves her into a situation where she uses what she has learnt, controls it and wallows in a variety of ideas. She has never stayed to school lunch, but she brings together these experiences so that they are integrated; so that she can deal with them safely – moving in and out of reality and non-reality.

Diya (five years) plays 'orphanages' with her dolls and soft toys. She dresses them all, and sits them round a pretend table. She rings a bell – 'Don't ask for more, 'cos you won't get it,' she says sternly to the teddy. She 'walks' some of the dolls round, clearing and wiping the table. She makes them all line up, blows a whistle, and sends them to school. Here is an integration of ideas, feelings and relationships. She has heard of orphanages in Romania, and seen the conditions on television news. She has heard and seen the film of 'Oliver', having been terrified by Nancy's murder scene. She has recently started at a reception class in an infant school, and is coming to terms with lining up for break, lunch, assembly, hometime, and PE (hence the whistle). She has started school meals, and has learnt about clearing tables.

Hannah, Sophie, Harry, and Emily are 10 years old. They play 'detectives', having read Agatha Christie. One sits in the room and interviews suspects. They demonstrate their understanding, and apply what they know of this style of drama and genre of literature. All their learning about this is applied. They dress up in character, having discussed general directions before beginning to free-flow. It takes about 10 minutes before they are sufficiently sensitive to each other, but they then move into the higher gear of rich free-flow play.

Marc (six years) and Chris (six and a half years) free-flow play with bicycles. They agree a circuit route, which involves difficult jumps and turns. They do not say they are performers, but their style and body gestures suggest it. They use what they know of recently seeing a police motor bike demonstration, watching older boys and girls in the park, and seeing films on television. It all comes together, as they use their technical prowess and wallow in their personal performances – 'as if' they are, to use their words, 'wicked' and the 'greatest'.

Conclusion

Increasingly, our knowledge makes us more careful with our terminology. If we are serious about showing why we value free-flow play with parents, colleagues and the public, we must be careful to signal what is and is not 'play', in the strictest sense. We shall need to 'do' and 'take part' in games, rather than 'play' them. Sometimes we shall play with clay, sometimes we shall represent and keep hold of experiences by making models. Margaret Clark (1988) stresses that those outside early years education often do not understand the importance of play. Terminology is therefore of crucial importance in sharing what we know with colleagues, parents and beyond. The word 'play', as Gardner (1982) suggests, is too broad and all pervasive. We need to narrow it down, or it will not be useful.

In this chapter, we have examined 12 features which help us to identify more effectively the nature of free-flow play.

The essence of these is formulated in the equation:

Free-flow play = wallow + competence

In the next two chapters, we shall look at some processes related to free-flow play, which although inter-related, remain separate in important ways.

5   Firsthand Experiences – the bedrock of free-flow play

Introduction to firsthand experience

In the last chapter, we established the features of free-flow play, and expressed their essence in an equation. This equation helps us, in this chapter, to see the major contribution of firsthand experience as the bedrock of free-flow play.

Free flow play = wallowing in ideas, + using the
                   feelings and   competence and
                   relationships   technical prowess
                                         that has been
                                         developed

Without firsthand experience, we cannot wallow in ideas, or feelings or relationships. Without direct and real experiences, we have no opportunities to develop our competence or technical prowess in a variety of ways.

We shall see that as we experience, so we struggle, manipulate, explore, discover and practise, in order to wallow fully, and become proficient. We are then in a position to free-flow play. As Bruner (1968, p. 118) points out, 'We get interested in what we get good at. In general, it is difficult to sustain interest in an activity unless one achieves some degree of competence'. Although at first we struggle, as we manipulate, explore, and discover, we repeat and practise. This develops competence. We see this in specific skills (e.g. fencing) and also in a general context (being nimble and having quick physical reactions).

If we can use firsthand experience as a means towards wallowing in experiences, and being proficient, we have a sense of control over our lives. We have seen how Catherine Garvey stresses the importance of this in free-flow play. This sense of control impinges upon self-esteem, self-confidence, autonomy, intrinsic motivation, the desire to have a go, to take risks and to solve problems, and the ability to make decisions and to choose. It is, therefore, important that children are offered rich and powerful firsthand experiences, and that they are actively helped by adults to make full use of them. Children make use of and apply firsthand experience when they free-flow play. Rich free-flow play occurs when children function at the highest levels of which they are capable.

The struggle of carrying three buckets.

Struggle occurs before free-flow play emerges

Tom (three and a half years), Hannah (six years), Katie (five and a half years) and Charlotte (three years) were playing 'gibbons' after a visit to the zoo. They were in the park on climbing frames. They swung from rung to rung, or at least, they tried to. It was too difficult. The attempt at free-flow play broke down because they did not have the physical competence to carry out their ideas.

Children do not develop competence whilst they free-flow play ('gibbons', or whatever). This happens beforehand in other contexts, and that is why it is important for adults to be on hand to help children at times of struggle, i.e. learning to swing on the climbing frame. We can actively and directly teach techniques which help children to swing, etc. This is then used spontaneously and without adult pressure in the child's free-flow play. Children need help whilst they struggle. If it is not forthcoming, they learn to avoid certain situations – or to have temper tantrums – and to give up when the going gets tough. Learning to roll pastry, to ride a bike, to tie a shoelace, to use glue, to use scissors, that there can be different versions to a story – these all require a sensitive adult, who recognises the teachable moment and swiftly moves in to give direct teaching, so that the child in due course can both wallow and become competent in these experiences.

Struggle occurs often when we have little prior experience to draw upon

Peter (10 months) has difficulty putting a spoon of food into his mouth. Imogen (two years) does not – or cannot – keep the paint in the pot. It tips. Charlie (three years) falls off his bike frequently. Nikolai (four years) accuses an adult of getting the story wrong – (he has not yet experienced different versions of it).

We need to remember that a young three year old has only a little more than half the experience of an old four year old, and that a young four year old has experienced only a little more than two thirds that of an old five year old (Clark, 1988). These are serious considerations when placing four year olds (some 80 per cent of them, according to Pascal, 1990) in formal infant classes which stress paper, pencils, and sitting at the table, more than direct, firsthand experiences – or making use of this through free-flow play. Gordon Wells (1987) points out that formal schooling causes great difficulty for many children. This is because it does not form a natural link with their home and cultural experiences. If we cannot find familiar links between our experiences, we struggle.

Struggle can cause damage

(a) Finding an appropriate curriculum

Because young children have comparatively so little experience, they need an appropriate curriculum that offers them basic firsthand experiences and demands educative and extending struggle, rather than damaging struggle. Traditional nursery education does this, and the British Nursery School has been admired and emulated throughout the world. This is because its curriculum is appropriate for children in the first seven years, although it is only in Denmark that children are kept in a nursery school environment until the age of seven. It is, however, interesting to note that in Denmark, there is very little adult illiteracy. This, linked with typical longitudinal studies in the USA and GB (Berruta *et al.*, 1984; Miller and Bizzell, 1983; and Osborn and Milbank, 1987) suggests that the long-term benefits of this type of curriculum, with its emphasis on open-ended firsthand experience and free-flow play, are great. Struggle is encouraged; the sort that encourages deep learning. Damaging struggle is avoided in this curriculum.

The All Party Parliamentary Select Committee on Provision for Under Fives (1989) condemned the practice of placing four year olds in early reception classes in infant schools, which constrains and cuts short firsthand experience. It often leads to struggle, causing anxiety (Clark, 1988). The 'Get them in and get them on' approach described by Shirley Cleave and Sandra Brown (1989, NFER) undervalues and indeed limits the firsthand experience which brings educative struggle.

Children might survive a curriculum which demands inappropriate struggle (lining up, lunchtimes, changing for PE – adult-led tasks predominating), but they are unlikely to flourish in the long term, as the research evidence suggests.

PJ (four years) found a dead bird in the nursery garden. He wondered why it was stiff. He had to struggle to fit this in with his understanding that birds are floppy, and was helped to do so by the teacher through conversations, developing an interest table around the bird, and through information books.

Gemma (four years) sat in assembly with the whole school (four to eleven year olds). They sang, 'There is a Green Hill Far Away, Without a City Wall'. This puzzled her. Why say it didn't have a wall? She had never seen a town *with* a wall. She was required to sit in silence for half an hour, and was reprimanded for talking and fidgeting. It did not occur to her to talk to the teacher about the song, because the atmosphere expected her to take up teacher-led experiences, rather than to dwell on hers.

(b) Strategies that cause children to avoid struggle

Dweck and Legett's (1988) research suggests that children either develop 'learning goals' or 'achievement goals'. Achievement goals lead children to try to gain favourable judgements from others – often teachers. They need to 'win', and they are likely to select tasks so that they can outperform. They develop very little sense of control, attributing success to ability, rather than to effort. They need to win because it makes them feel they might have ability. They avoid struggle.

Jack (four years) is in an infant class of 30 children and one teacher. Children are set different tasks at different tables. Jack is on the fish-making table. He is to select a template, draw round it, cut it out, and draw the eyes, etc. He is then to stick on milk bottle tops for scales, and to make a fringe of tissue paper to stick on as a tail. The fish do not resemble any species – they are fantasy fish.

Jack chooses a fat template, because it is easier to hold and draw round. He does not overlap his milk bottle tops. He would like to, because he knows that is what fish scales are like. It is, however, too difficult to make it look good this way, and he wants his fish to be put on the wall, as 'good work'. He would really like to make a goldfish, but there isn't any orange tissue paper on the table.

Jack wants external signs of success. There is no adult available to help him to put in the struggle and effort necessary in striving for personal standards of success. Low-level activities – such as tracing, templates, stencils and the screwed-up tissue paper syndrome, often used to fill in template outlines – encourage children to experience external success and to avoid struggle.

It is not in children's interests to give them successes with low-level activities, because these leave them without the ownership and the self-esteem to believe in themselves as creators. They deny them control, and discourage them from the effort of struggling. This has a long-term detrimental impact on learning and development.

(c) Effects of ridiculing or mocking children

If children are ridiculed or mocked when they struggle, they will become cautious about putting themselves in struggle settings. This in turn will have an impact on intrinsic motivation and autonomy, e.g. a two year old putting boots on the wrong feet. Children learn to avoid struggle when they are constantly unsupported through it, and so do not develop the competence they need for free-flow play and high-level functioning.

Supported struggle can be a catalyst to development, and so to free-flow play

(a) Learning rather than achievement goals

Dweck's research points out the dangers of avoiding struggle through achievement goals, and demonstrates the benefits of helping children to struggle towards 'learning goals'. These involve a concern for personal competence and ways of increasing mastery. They concern struggle, leading to personal standards of success.

Darren (four years) had spent the morning making a record player. He had a box, with control knobs, and a straw for the needle and bar. He wanted a perfect black circle for the record, in order to complete it. He struggled to draw the circle. It was story time, but the teacher said he could finish his model, recognising its importance for him. Whilst reading the story, she began to realise he was at a struggle level on the last stage of the model.

He nearly had a temper tantrum. She rushed to him, asking the nursery nurse to take over the story quick! There was not time to explain. She just got there in time to stop him from breaking up his model. She helped him to make three records to go on his record player. He calmed down, and he experienced success. Because the teacher and nursery nurse worked in partnership, the whole group did not suffer, and neither did Darren.

It is interesting to note this would have been more difficult if Darren had been in an early reception class with only one adult. Either Darren, the whole class or both would have suffered, and valuable learning would have been lost. Children need support through struggle – they cannot be left alone – or they will learn to avoid it, and experience a feeling of incompetence. This will not encourage them in the valuable learning goals that Dweck describes.

[b] A secure environment

When children meet new objects and new people, they need the support and encouragement of those significant to them, so that they are not left anxiously to struggle. Corinne Hutt demonstrated that young children need a secure setting if they are to struggle with new actions and ideas.

Jamie (six months) watches his mother while he manipulates and explores a wooden spoon, a plastic kite spool, a bracelet, a thermos flask lid and a small wooden tube of bamboo. He is in a new room, and there are strangers in it – people he has never met. He looks at his mother every time someone new appears. (It is a gathering of adults and children.) She smiles and picks up the spoon, saying, 'Do you want this?', using the typical high-register voice of a mother. Reassured, he explores again.

We struggle when situations do not conform to our expectations

Tom (three years) saw a yellow beetle which looked like a ladybird. It didn't fit with what he knew; that sort of beetle should be red. This struggle was interesting although other situations involving struggle to adjust to the unexpected can cause anxiety. Maisie (one year) screams when she sees someone wearing face paints. This is not what faces should be like. Adjusting our thinking, struggling to deal with the unexpected, is an emotional experience. Fiona (four years) can cut paper proficiently. She uses this skill in cutting some metal wrapping paper, but it only dents. She has to stuggle (helped by her teacher) to develop her technique in making a cut in it. She has to tilt the blade more than when cutting paper. As Richard Feynman (1990) says, 'The thing that doesn't fit is the most interesting'.

Manipulation, exploration and discovery

Open ended activities – a catalyst for high-level representation and free-flow play

Darren was involved in an open-ended activity: he decided to make the record player. He decided which materials to use. He struggled to complete what he set out to do, and he received help when the going got tough. He saw the rewards of his struggle – an exceptionally good model, which has moving parts. A by-product was everyone's admiration. Children know real admiration from patronising admiration. He told people where he received help, which is typical of children in this kind of classroom. This kind of manipulation, exploration and discovery of materials that are directly experienced leads into possibilities for free-flow play, and – in this case – a representational model, which could be a prop for free-flow play.

Helen McAuley examined adult-led tasks, such as those recommended by Hughes (1986), in helping children to develop in early number work. She concluded that these are certainly high-level and challenging for young children. However, she points out (1990, p. 122):

> There is some doubt that such a specific and highly challenging sort of activity is more likely to foster active, creative learning than the broader based activities which may appear to be less challenging but which the individual child can with adult help use profitably as a springboard for more challenging work.

It depends where our priorities lie. We need to look at ourselves, and to examine what these are.

McAuley suggests that open-ended provision helps children, as they manipulate, explore and discover, in ways which they can then use as a 'springboard' into the process of free-flow play that is creative and challenging. She draws on the work of Sestini (1987), Athey (1981) and Duckworth (1979) to support this. Classrooms need to encourage children through being self-servicing, as workshop environments, so that children can actively select and choose as they manipulate, explore and discover.

Closed tasks – a catalyst for low-level representation and free-flow play

Jack was involved in a closed, pre-structured task. It was someone else's idea to make a fish. It was someone else's representation of a fish. Where is Jack in all this? He can operate at a low level, and he opts for an even lower level in deciding that it must look good, and has the satisfaction of seeing it go up on the wall. He is learning to aim for public praise. He is not in control of his ideas. He is unlikely to become an autonomous learner; instead, he will learn to please the teacher.

The long-term research studies mentioned above suggest that children in programmes with a skills-orientated approach typically begin to do less well in school from junior school onwards.

A Scottish early years teacher on an Advanced Diploma Course at Moray House College, who had previously organised pre-structured tasks for children (seven years) and a tightly run routine, had moved into a 'free-choice' approach, with careful record keeping, so that she could monitor children's individual needs and act on her observations. She worked hard to provide a wide range of firsthand experiences through which children could manipulate, explore and discover. She noted in her file that she looked round the room after six weeks, and for the first time did not feel guilty about pausing in order to observe the children. She had begun to realise that this was an important part of her teaching. She found a room full of children actively learning, instead of a room full of children being taught. She liked what she saw.

The role of the adult – good observers, sensitive
to the child

Each of us has implicit views about learning. Inevitably,
these emerge as we work with children. We have seen two
strands developing, even though both place free-flow play
centrally in education. One stresses the outcomes of play;
the other stresses the processes of play, with the rich spin-
off of equipping the child for future life.

Kit (eight years) was given a half-term project of making a
collage. He was not used to such open-ended activities in
the school he attended – a new teacher had arrived – and he
kept putting it off. His aunt, a nursery teacher, offered to
help him. He needed a subject. She asked him about books,
outings, television programmes, etc. He said he was
enjoying *Journey to the Centre of the Earth*. They chatted.
He liked the dinosaurs. They narrowed it down – he really
liked the pterodactyls. So far, so good. He began to bite his
nails as they started to ponder how to do this in a collage.

Kit's aunt asked him whether he wanted to use manu-
factured materials (plastic, etc.) or natural. He loves
science, and perked up. He made a collection in the garden
of natural objects, from moss and bark, to leaves and stones.
He became depressed – they wouldn't stick: 'I'd better use
tissue paper'. 'No!', said his aunt, who had a horror of the
screwed-up tissue paper syndrome. 'Keep going. We need
strong glue.' They went to the shop and had a happy time
discussing glues. They decided 'glues' should be his
birthday present in advance.

Whilst they were shopping, his aunt dropped thoughts
into the conversation: it would be nice to use the leaf veins
– they would look like wings, etc. By the time Kit returned
with the glue, he had many possibilities to try out in his
collage. He could select from these and use them for
himself. He spent two hours, selecting and rearranging. His
aunt only needed to make supportive remarks, e.g. 'Another
idea bites the dust!' – to signal that errors are exciting. This
encouraged Kit to keep going. He had his lunch on a tray
while he worked. His aunt stayed near. He made a beautiful
collage of a prehistoric scene. He was deeply satisfied, and
it brought genuine admiration from the family.

Typically, Kit pointed out where he had received help,
because, in the main, it was his, and he felt ownership as its
creator. He realised that he did have good ideas and he did

have the courage to manipulate, explore and discover using the materials he gathered.

The need to practise

Gradually, as adjustments are made, the struggle aspect lessens. The spoon goes into the mouth, the paint stays in the pot and goes onto the paper in the way intended by the child, the grazes from falling off the bike are less frequent, and stories are looked at to see how they differ in endings, etc. It is during this time that children practise. They repeat, over and over again, and they need a wide range of opportunities to do this. They develop a wealth of ideas in which they can later wallow in their free-flow play.

When children repeat, they are learning in quite a direct way. Traditionally, nursery education has always given children a wealth of opportunities to do this. However, whilst the struggle stage requires constant and 100 per cent full-time support from adults or more advanced peers, the practice stage of repetition does not require such full-time direct interaction, and may often need only indirect support, wherein lies the strength of the indirectly structured early childhood curriculum (Tamburrini, in Richards, 1982).

If children are simply left to themselves, in a *laissez-faire* environment, they become involved in stereotyped, repetitious play, e.g. with sand and water (Hutt, 1982) or blocks (Gura, ed., directed by Bruce, 1992, in press). Just putting out basic equipment is not enough. It leaves too much responsibility with the child, who may well be too inexperienced to take on such responsibility. On the other hand, filling in worksheets with rows of practice sums or letters undermines the ability to initiate, take risks or be confident outside that setting. It leads quickly to children saying, 'I can't draw a circle'.

Practising without boredom

Hebb gives a helpful approach to practice and its value. He talks about the importance of 'difference in sameness'. Children need to be able to repeat in order to consolidate their learning, and so become competent and proficient in it. There needs to be paint, etc., constantly available, but not always set out in the same way – sometimes an easel, or the flat of the floor, etc., to work on. In this way, interest is maintained during the stage of repetition. It encourages deeper exploration and manipulation.

Interactive interest tables, and displays which grow organically, make a shared experience for the group, and provide opportunities to repeat in a variety of ways.

Rich and broad provision in order to practise effectively

Children operate at different levels in different situations. A popular misinterpretation of Piagetian theory is that children operate at the same level (e.g. sensori-motor level) across the board. This is not what Piaget said, nor is it commonsense. Development is not linear in this way. It is uneven and has jagged edges, as we shall see when we look at Chaos Theory in Chapter 7. Children need to do the same things using many different materials. They can make a rotation by pirouetting, by drawing or painting a circle, or by turning a screwdriver. It becomes a different experience each time the materials are changed, even though it always involves rotation in some form or another. Children need access to a wide variety of materials all of the time, or they do not fully experience, for example, rotation in all its aspects.

Alice Honig (1985) emphasises that we need to 'dance the developmental ladder'. As she points out, this tends to be more pronounced where children have special educational needs (McConkey, in Smith, 1986). For example, Carol (nine years), who contracted meningitis at two, functions in many respects at the level of her peers, but she cannot read, and shows no interest in writing or stories.

The environment needs to be set up to allow practice at different levels across different activities and media. The traditional early childhood environment found particularly in nursery schools achieves this. It has its indoor and outdoor provision, space, and the high adult/child ratio which is crucial in helping children to use these areas (Osborne and Milbank, 1987; Clark, 1988). Some children will be playing with sand; others will be struggling with getting to know it – learning not to throw into eyes, or clap hands to shake it off. Others will be exploring it; by making dry sand into a castle; trying it wet; seeing if it happens today like it did yesterday. Are its properties constant? Will it have the same effect in this bucket as that cup?

Materials need to be non-toxic, in case children smell or eat them, or get trapped inside things, etc. An American friend once described this as a 'yes' environment.

Double provision

Double provision means having, for example, two home corners, two sand trays, etc. Double provision, from time to time – and where practically possible – provides opportunities for different levels of practice and avoids the problems of the stereotyped play that the Hutts' research (1970s) dwells upon. One child can tip and pour water in the water tray, whilst another can experiment with different materials and investigate their absorbency, or use the play people and boats to make a complicated narrative without pots and splashes constraining its development.

Exploring the feel of clay.

Some element of double provision also overcomes the problems of what we might call the 'dough on a Monday' syndrome. In order to give children a wealth of different experiences, there may be dough: Monday, red clay: Tuesday, white clay: Wednesday, bread baking: Thursday and Friday: plasticine (because it's easier to clear up for the weekend!). This takes no account of individual children's needs. It simply puts them through a programme of activities. In contrast, sometimes making double provision allows for breadth of activities as a general principle, and means that if Shanaz (four years) needs more time practising to make clay do as she wishes, this can be provided, to give her the experience she needs to repeat and consolidate her learning. Children need to sing a song many times before they know it. They need to use clay many times before they can make it do what they want. In this way, the needs of the group and of the individual can be catered for.

Another aspect of double provision operates in the indoor and outdoor settings. Anything a child does indoors, they should be able to do outdoors. Indoors, they might draw with crayons, pens, etc; outdoors, with a bucket of water and a large brush on the walls. All too often, outdoors is not regarded as anything more than a place for excess energy. On the contrary, it can provide opportunities for a range of experiences through which to practise (e.g. drawing).

Practice makes perfect

Good swingers tend to hang from banisters, which may not be strong, and use 'gibbons' sound effects, which can be hard on adult nerves. Those good with the scissors may use them in their play in ways which upset adults, e.g. Hannah (four years), who could cut shapes with scissors, also cut a zig-zag line along Tom's (18 months) fringe whilst playing hairdressers. Barbara (four years) was heard to remark, 'Just right for my Rosie' and put a circular rag on her doll's head for a hat. She had cut it from the back of an armchair cover at home.

It is important to note that these three examples are from home settings. Supervision is such in education and care settings that potential events can be more easily spotted in advance. There would be a junk area for Barbara to select material. There might be old wigs for Hannah to trim. There would be climbing frames and other children to become gibbons with in the outdoor area. It is not nearly as satisfying to be a gibbon alone. One of the great strengths of nursery education is that it is geared towards providing children with opportunities for firsthand experience, which they can use in their play in ways that are acceptable. For many reasons, this is not always easy at home, especially for those in bed-and-breakfast accommodation.

An overview of firsthand experience

1   Because they are young, children have not experienced as much as adults. Maslow (1962, p. 87–8) believes that one major experience that catches the mind and the emotion is worth a thousand pedestrian ones. It is important that we offer children experiences they can use and value as their lives move forward.

2   The provision we make indoors and outdoors is of central importance. Through this context we offer children firsthand experiences that are appropriate, supportive and extending.

3   The role of adults is crucial in helping children to take up opportunities for firsthand experiencing, so that they gain access to high levels of functioning, as in free-flow play.

When children *struggle*, they tackle the unfamiliar and the unexpected. They need us to be there, actively and directly helping them. When children *manipulate, explore* and *discover*, they need less direct help. They need indirect help as we extend provision, and converse with them (Tamburrini, 1981), rather than monologues at them (Wells, 1987).

When children *practise*, they also need less direct help. Indirect help requires an adult who is informed about child development, the curriculum context and content, and who can interact sensitively with children.

4   Firsthand experience gives children a basis for wallowing in the ideas, feelings and relationships they make use of in free-flow play.

5   It also helps them to develop the competence they

require, in order to indulge in high levels of free-flow play.

Conclusion

Corinne and John Hutt (1990) distinguish between epistemic or exploratory play, and ludic or free-flow play (imaginative, free play). They argue that ludic play does not involve children in learning, unlike epistemic play. Bennett and Kell (1989) doubt the benefits of free-flow play, and stress teacher-led tasks.

There is a danger that this might lead us to believe that we should only involve children in a curriculum where they learn all the time. As we have seen in the last section, this stance is too simplistic. Learning can be direct or indirect, and firsthand experience involves children in both. Direct input does not have to mean pre-structured tasks, and Helen McAuley (1990, p. 118) suggests that these 'so-called "high challenge" activities do not either necessarily match and stimulate the learner, nor provide an experience which will facilitate characteristics of learning such as creativity, imagination, reflective and critical thinking which teachers often aim to encourage'. Open-ended situations give children input of firsthand experience, which may be of more use to children's learning than pre-structured activities.

In contrast, free-flow play is an example of the way that children apply, use and integrate the inputs of firsthand experiences. As Vygotsky (1978, p. 101) reminds us, free-flow play is not the only means by which children apply their learning, but it is as he suggests, a central one. It enables children to be free from practical constraints, so that they can function at their very highest levels. Not only does free-flow play take children to perform at the highest level of which they are capable, it is a catalyst to the development of games, humour and representation. We shall see how in the next chapter. In this chapter, we have seen that without rich firsthand experiences, which give input by supporting and extending children, there would be no possibility for free-flow play.

6 Games, Humour and Representation

The network of processes for which free-flow play is a catalyst

We saw in the last chapter that firsthand experience is of central importance in a child's development. Particularly, it offers children opportunities to struggle, manipulate, explore, discover and to become competent and proficient through practice and consolidation. Firsthand experiences – rather than television or stories, which are secondary – act as the bedrock for free-flow play, which leads children to wallow in ideas, feelings and relationships. Firsthand experiences also give children opportunities to apply the technical competencies they have developed.

In turn, free-flow play acts as a catalyst for rich development of games, humour, representation and decentration. For all of these situations – exploring, free-flow play, representation, etc. – Helen McAuley (1990, p. 120) emphasises that 'to make really adequate provision, the individual child must be closely observed, listened to and taken seriously'. Firsthand experiences, via struggle, manipulation, exploration, discovery and practice, form the basis of free-flow play, games, humour, representation and decentration. In this chapter, we shall see how these processes form a network; each linking with the other, yet separate and unique (see Figure 1, below).

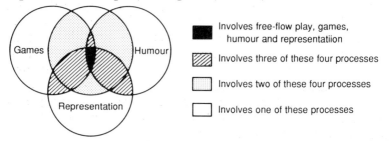

Figure 1 *Free-flow play – a catalyst to games, humour and representation.*

At times, free-flow play moves into – and even becomes – representation; and then moves back to being free-flow play. Free-flow play is rarely present in an entirely pure form, with all 12 features.

In the same way, as agreed rules become more dominant, free-flow play develops into a game, and then often returns to being free-flow play once more, as the Opies (1988) observed in their study of children's street games. The rules are sometimes conventional and shared, but often they become idiosyncratic and personal to the children involved. At other times, humour enters into the seriousness of free-flow play, with wit and jokes dominating, and then fading into deep serious thinking again.

At times, free-flow play is difficult to distinguish from other related processes, such as games, humour and representation; sometimes it is easy to distinguish between these. If adults strive to take out the similarities and differences between these processes, it becomes easier to help children participate in the rule behaviour of their culture (Bruner, 1990), to develop a good sense of humour (Athey, 1976), and to richly represent their own experiences (Matthews, 1988). The 12 features of free-flow play (see p. 59) help us to see what is pure play, and what is less distinct.

Games

Games have agreed rule formats

Games can have many of the features of free-flow play, but have externally generated rules and goals (Feature 3). They help children to link the personal and idiosyncratic rule structures of free-flow play with the more formal and symbolic rules of situations, as understood by others participating in the culture. Games have clear rule formats, and the understanding of and participation in games helps children to become a part of their particular culture, bridging their personal and action-based rule formats with those of their society. Conversations, formal greetings and partings, Parliamentary debates, meetings with Royalty, are all games with rule formats.

There are many types of game, and each is important for the child's full participation in his/her culture.

Bruner and games

Bruner has looked particularly at the games which help children towards conversations. Peter (nine months) takes part in a Peek-a-boo game with his sister, Sophie (four years). 'There is turn taking, hider and hidden, actor and experiencer, and an ordered sequence of events' (Bruner, 1983, p. 4).

As Bruner points out, such games are often playful and fun. However, this does not mean that they involve the child in free-flow playing. In his view, such games initiate the child into the abstract and symbolic layers of behaviour in his/her culture. Every culture involves children in games which will lead them further and further into life within that culture.

> Our culturally adapted way of life depends upon shared meanings and shared concepts and depends as well upon shared modes of discourse for negotiating differences in meaning and interpretation . . . the child does not enter the life of his or her group as a private and artistic sport of primary processes, but rather as a participant in a larger public process in which public meanings are negotiated (Bruner, 1990, p. 13).

As we have seen in Chapter 2, Bruner identifies games, playfulness and play. He is ill at ease about the value of too much free-flow play with sand, bikes or rough and tumble. It is too private and individual. This is because there is no clear rule format, initiating the child into the culture.

In Piaget's and Vygotsky's theories, this lack of a clear rule format is not seen as a problem in free-flow play in the early years. Vygotsky argues (1978, p. 94), 'The imaginary situation of any form of play already contains rules of behaviour, although it may not be a game with formulated rules laid down in advance'. However, Vygotsky does see free-flow play gradually turning into games, with rules laid down, as does Piaget. In free-flow play, the child is like 'an unsuccessful algebraist who cannot yet write down the symbols but can depict them in action'. Bruner, Vygotsky and Piaget all stress the importance of games in development, either from the start (Bruner) or from approximately seven years, when children can use agreed symbols (Piaget and Vygotsky). Vygotsky and Piaget are more in favour of free-flow play in the early years – e.g. rough and tumble, or with sand and water – than Bruner. This is because they see it as enabling children to use action-based and personal rule formats, which precede formal, agreed and shared symbols.

However, it may not be useful to see participation in games with shared, conventional rules as superior to the personal, idiosyncratic rules, and use of shared experience, of free-flow play. Free-flow play acts as a powerful mechanism through which children distinguish different kinds of rule behaviour; primarily through acting directly on personal, idiosyncratic rules, and at times sharing these through similar experience.

Some different types of games

We have briefly examined games expressed as cultural rituals, greetings, partings, etc., in which there is a set of agreed rules which help those taking part to know in advance how to behave. Bruner (1990, p. 2) points out that these 'focused upon the symbolic activities that human beings employed in constructing and in making sense, not only of the world, but of themselves'. In the classroom setting, these are, of course, important. However, a type of game which has become dominant is the mathematical game.

1   Mathematical games

Martin Hughes (1986, p. 134), looking at numbers, shows how we can help children to 'use the conventional written symbols of arithmetic'. He argues that mathematical games help in 'introducing young children to formal arithmetical symbolism'.

Hughes applies three principles, involving continuity, empowerment and cultural resonance. Continuity means building up personal knowledge. This makes use of what the child has learnt directly through firsthand experience, and what the child can apply. It introduces children to the language of games (in this case, mathematical language), and it links them with their culture's way of going about things in ways which hold meaning for them, e.g. in playing chess, Monopoly, snakes and ladders.

2   Performance games: the rules of an exact advance script

There are some games which have an exact advance script, or a definite shape, text, notation or composition that lays down strict rules for performance. We could call these situations 'performance' games. In performing choreographed dance music or a drama (e.g. the Chinese Opera, Indian classical dance, the ballet Giselle), not a move or expression must be out of place. We are interpreting someone else's symbols and there are rules to be obeyed. When we use symbols in writing, musical composition, or dance choreography, we also take part in a culturally agreed game. There are agreed rules in writing sonnets, or a Japanese Haiku poem, rap, or performing the school Christmas nativity play. It is not appropriate to require young children to take part in such performance games in a public setting, with an audience largely unknown to them. Children need to create their own advance scripts, to share with those who are significant to them before performing them to unknown spectators.

3   Sports games

Here the rules are explicit and generally agreed, but the shape of the game depends on the interaction of the participants as much as the rules, e.g. fencing, football. In this respect, sports games are like mathematical games (e.g. chess). A good game has rules which allow for plenty of scope in interaction, e.g. to win the Under 11s fencing competition, Tom needs to know the rules of the fencing game. He also needs to tune into the thinking and mood of his opponent, to anticipate, surprise, and overcome surprises through a wide repertoire of possible moves. In a game like fencing, the agreed rules predominate more than in free-flow play settings.

When games become free-flow play, and the reverse

Catherine Garvey raises some important distinctions between games and free-flow play, which help us to see how near to each other they become at times. Free-flow play may move into a game. 'You're not playing properly,' Chris (seven years) accuses David (five years). They had agreed that David would have the part of running up the slope to fend off attackers, but he has broken from the advance script. However, although there are agreed rules between them, this is still free-flow play. As Catherine Garvey (1977, p. 102) points out, games are 'structured by explicit rules that can be precisely communicated'. The rules of this free-flow play were constantly shifting, as is typical of this kind of play. This is why it burgeons, fades, returns, etc.

When children are getting to know one another, they often use the explicit rules of a game fairly rigidly. As we have seen, games are about getting to know the rules of a culture and its layers of symbols. In this sense, they are 'Acts of Meaning' (Bruner, 1990); they are about getting to know people in a culture, as part of it. In the following example, the game of Monopoly helped Hannah and Mikael through an awkward 'getting to know you' period. For this reason, games are also played at parties, because they make groups who do not know each other well feel secure in unfamiliar settings.

Mikael (13 years) and Hannah (13 years) are on an exchange visit. Mikael has just arrived in England, and is nervous about his ability to speak English. Hannah is equally nervous about speaking French. They both know the game Monopoly. This game makes them feel secure. They know what is expected, can predict, plan and feel in control in a definite direction, with a definite game. They can practise, and become more proficient at it. Games reassure us that what we thought was so, is so. They also encourage us to 'push the rules' to the limits, to see what happens – e.g. tennis, chess, football, snooker, John Cage's music, e. e. Cummings' poetry.

When we push the rules, we move almost imperceptably into free-flow play. Mikael and Hannah stuck to the rules of the game Monopoly in order to feel secure. In contrast, the children who lived in the same street and knew each other well, in the Opies' study of singing games (Opie and Opie, 1988), made variations on a theme. The game served as an agreed, rough advance script, and was changed as they went along, i.e. moving into free-flow play (Garvey, 1977, p. 102). When children free-flow play, the Opies (1988, p. 30) point out, 'Since the games are their own they can play them with affectionate disrespect'. The games no longer have definite directions, and so gently move back into free-flow play.

Catherine Garvey stresses that free-flow play is a dialogue with the environment. In order for this to occur, there must be some rules, but the extent to which these dominate determines whether we are taking part in a game; with a clear sense of direction, or free-flow play, without a specific direction or shape. Free-flow play is more organic in its growth. Where the two move closely towards each other, we see some of the highest levels of human functioning.

> The creative act, by connecting previously unrelated dimensions of experience, enables him to attain to a high level of mental evolution. It is an act of liberation, the defeat of habit by originality (Koestler, 1976, p. 96).

Externally agreed rules create cultural habits. It is when we look at these again, and think afresh about them, that creativity, originality and imagination can develop. This is when we free-flow play.

Free-flow play as a catalyst to games

Let us remind ourselves of Catherine Garvey's suggestion that only the lower species adhere to an exact script, or rules, with an exact direction. We have established that the shared rules of games are important as acts of meaning within a culture, but we have also come to see that the ability to make variations on the rules, and to change the games, is equally important. Games are not the same as free-flow play. Neither does free-flow play inevitably turn into games. Neither are games superior to free-flow play. As Sara Similanski (1968, p. 59) points out, children of five to six years old can take part in games competently, without having free-flow played. The development of socio-dramatic play – the aspect of free-flow play that she studies – is not considered to be a prerequisite for the later stage of games with rules.

However, we are hoping to find ways to help children in their learning and development as broadly and deeply as possible, so that they operate beyond a minimal, or survival, level, and flourish. All games and no free-flow play means all competence and technical prowess, with little 'pushing the rules' into variations on a theme, alternative ideas, wallowing in ideas, individuality, creativity, originality, innovation or imagination.

Free-flow play is not a prerequisite to games. It is a separate process. It is, however, a powerful catalyst to the development of games. To return to Tom and Nikolai and their fencing, they can be imaginative fencers, or not. The hours of free-flow play spent in their pre-fencing days – pretending to be medieval archers, throwing javelins (sticks) into a bush in the garden, aiming paper aeroplanes, being Robin Hood and aiming swords, bows and arrows as they demonstrated their increasing technical prowess and rich ideas to wallow with – have helped them to take part both imaginatively and with technique in the game of fencing.

It may well be that some of us are more drawn towards taking part in games (Gascoigne the footballer, Steve Davis the snooker player, Kasparov the chess player, Markova the ballet dancer), whilst others are driven towards free-flow play (e.g. research scientists like Einstein or Feynman, or artists like Leonardo da Vinci or Isadora Duncan, who knew how to ignore or break pre-set rules). Perhaps this simply reflects different personalities. However, we need both, and when the balance between games and free-flow play is optimal, we see exciting levels of technical prowess, combined with deeply imaginative endeavours, taking part in a culturally valued activity – e.g. when free-flow play finds a definite direction or purpose, it moves into becoming a game with explicit rules.

Summary of games

Games help children to understand rules that are explicitly structured, precisely communicated, and agreed upon. Through a balance of free-flow play and games, they come to understand how to make up rules and how to adhere to rules decided by others. They see the purpose and function of rules. They see that rules can be created, altered, abandoned or kept. They decentre, and look at the situation from different points of view.

Games can fulfil all the features of free-flow play, except that they have rules which lead to certain specific outcomes, e.g. to win a game of snooker, to sing and perform 'Brown Girl in the Ring'.

Humour

Humorous activity may or may not be free-flow play. When in the form of a repeated joke, it is clearly not, given the pressure of externally generated rules and direction. However, humorous activity can fulfil all 12 features of free-flow play. Chris Athey (in Chapman and Foot, 1977) sees this as the highest form of free-flow play, for it involves knowing something so well that it is possible to play with your play: e.g. in the Froebel Nursery Project (Athey, 1990, p. 200), five years olds found it amusing to play at pouring water into a sieve, knowing the water would go through the holes. Pretending to give a friend a cup of tea in this situation makes the activity hilarious to the players.

Kate (five years), Jonathan (four years) and Ellen (three years) were in the garden. The two guinea pigs were in a pen on the grass. One worked its way out of the pen, followed by the other. No-one noticed, but suddenly the three garden walls had four cats sitting on them, gazing intently, ready to spring. Tom sounded the alert, and everyone chased about, trying to fend off cats and catch guinea pigs. They were retrieved; the pen was mended; the cats disappeared.

A few days later, this group of children were again in the garden. They had made a den with blankets, trees and cushions. Suddenly, there were cushions being thrown, grabbed, and generally a rushing about. Someone climbed on a wall and pounced on a cushion on the ground, which was retrieved by someone else. There was convulsive laughter and delight. Then, as is typical of free-flow play, it began to fade, and they went into the den again. For a few minutes, it had held the atmosphere of the day the guinea pigs escaped. The children knew about carnivores and vegetarians, hunters and hunted, attacking and defence. They were playing, in a humorous way, with their knowlege of nature raw in tooth and claw.

This is free-flow play, in that it shows the 12 features. It is process rather than product orientated. The children are intrinsically motivated, with no external pressure to conform to specific rules; they are 'supposing', wallowing, using a shared experience, and decentring, as they look at the situation from different points of view. The play is sustained, competent, and child-initiated. It is in a group. It integrates their experience with the guinea pigs. However, it adds an extra dimension – humour.

Free-flow play does not always have this quality. It can be very serious. Erikson, Winnicott, Isaacs, Anna Freud and Melanie Klein developed the serious side of free-flow play through play therapy. In this way, with the help of the play therapist, children integrate, and deal with situations giving them pain (e.g. through a bereavement, through being abused). Normal free-flow play settings also do this, but most children do not require the specialist support of a play therapist, as they integrate painful experiences along-side pleasurable ones – e.g. the death of a guinea pig, an ice-cream falling on the floor, sitting on the cherished paper aeroplane, disappointment that a friend can't come to tea. Free-flow play in ordinary classroom settings, and in the home, helps children to deal with and integrate these experiences. However, when free-flow play develops humour, it offers something unique in the child's development. Koestler (1976), in the Introduction to *Act of Creation*, refers to 'the spontaneous flash of insight which shows a familiar situation or event in a new light'.

In this book, it has been stressed that children use free-flow play to mix, match and rearrange experiences. Humour means that the mixing, matching and rearranging is done to create comic incongruity. Rachel (five years) and Grace (four years) have an idea that boys do not wear frilly dresses. They dress Ben (18 months) in a blue, frilly dress and bonnet, and play mummies and daddies with him. They are in hysterics over this.

Chukovsky (1963)and Margaret Meek (1985) stress the importance of jokes and wit. These often take the form of spoken words. However, there is also situational humour. Children often make movements which show humour.

Summary of humour

Humorous activity may or may not be free-flow play, depending on whether it fulfils the 12 features. It is beneficial to all children if they can enjoy their ideas, as they rearrange, mix and match them, and create comic incongruities. As Koestler (1976, p. 120) points out, humour cannot come from nothing. Humour 'uncovers, selects, reshuffles, combines, synthesises already existing facts, ideas, faculties, skills'. Free-flow play is where this takes place, and humour means that it is taking place at a very high level of functioning.

Representation

Bruner (1981) describes representation as the way we manage to keep hold of our own experiences in an orderly way. We shall see that representation can contain many, if not all, of the features of free-flow play; with the important exception that representation has a product, personal or publicly shared, which free-flow play does not (see the 12 features, p. 59). In exploring this difference between free-flow play and representation, we inevitably find ourselves looking at the way adults interact with children, for it is a key issue. We shall look at the adult's sensitivity in leaving free-flow play as a process without product; in nurturing emergent, personalised, idiosyncratic products; and in helping children to share and look critically at the products they are willing to make more public.

Shanaz (four years) had been to the zoo on a school outing. She went to the paint table, and using blue and red paint, made stripes on the paper. She did three stripey paintings. Then, she found some black and white striped material on the junk table. She glued it onto a piece of paper, and painted four legs in black. She said it was a zebra. Shanaz is representing. In terms of the 12 features, she is intrinsically motivated, under no pressure to conform to external rules, can paint 'as if', and wallow in her ideas, feelings and relationship with zebras. She is using firsthand experience in a sustained way. She is showing great technical prowess in her use of paint and collage. She is initiating the activity, and is working alone – though telling a sensitive adult what she has done. She is bringing together many aspects of her learning. The only difference between this and free-flow play is that she has made a product, through which she can keep hold of her zoo experience.

Adults must not try to force a product out of the child's free-flow play

Stephen (six years) and Roxanna (six years) were playing together. He initiated using the train set, and she brought the dolls house furniture and the dolls. They made villages along the track, and a story developed with dolls getting off and on trains, going visiting, shopping, etc. However, the story was not a product to be written down, or 'kept hold of', in the Brunerian sense. It was here and gone, and the free-flow play would have been spoilt if the adult had insisted on a product – such as making a book of the story. Adults can join free-flow play and participate in it. They can extend it through suggestions, conversations about it, and by providing appropriate props, materials, space and time for it. If they force a product out of free-flow play, they spoil it. This is more damaging than it seems, for children learn quickly to avoid this pressure to produce (and so often be judged) by not sharing their free-flow play. However, without adult help, free-flow play cannot develop as richly as it might. Stephen and Roxanna needed space, time and props for their free-flow play (J. and D. Singer, 1990) and appreciated a sensitive adult quietly acting as a catalyst to their needs. Without the pressure of having to produce 'a product', they had wider boundaries within which to develop their ideas. They were less constrained – and this, paradoxicaly, acted in the long term as a catalyst for rich representational products.

Free-flow play has no product. It ebbs and flows.

Adults are important in helping personal, idiosyncratic products to develop in representation

Throughout this book, it is stressed that free-flow play is often not pure in the form it takes. In other words, all 12 features are rarely present. There are times when free-flow play and representation come close together, especially in very young children. This is because early representations are very personal and idiosyncratic. They are only shared with people special to the child (Denny Tayler, 1984).

The adult who forces a product out of free-flow play is often the adult who forces these early personal products into the public domain. The adult in the following example was sensitive to Sadiq's personal representation, recognising that it was almost free-flow play. It was almost without product.

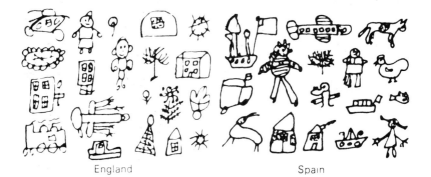

England   Spain

Egypt

Figure 2   The common forms children use universally to make their personal and idiosyncratic representations. (Source: The Crucial Years *ed. Daphne Plastow.)*

Vietnam

Germany

China

Sadiq (three years) went to the paint table. He did a splash painting. He had been fascinated at the zoo, watching the elephant have a bath. He sprayed the paint, his facial expression showing great pleasure. The teacher did not force the connection with the zoo trip by asking him, 'Are you painting the elephant having a bath?' (i.e. a product). Instead, she said, 'This reminds me of the elephant having a bath'. He turned, gave her a penetrating look and said, 'It is' (i.e. *he* decided it was a product, not the teacher). She realised it would be inappropriate to put this on the wall because it was private between them; but he took it home, and the teacher noticed that he told his mother.

We need to be careful before we put paintings on the wall. If they are free-flow play – or idiosyncratic, personal products – it is inappropriate to place them in the public eye.

Frank Smith (1985), in a lecture at the Institute of Education, University of London, made an important distinction. He gave the example of children writing, and showing chosen adults what they had written – in the spirit of wanting people to share admiration for their creations. This differs from the child showing the adult the writing in the spirit of someone asking an editor or publisher to scrutinise the manuscript with a view to possible publication. The former is not asking for critical comment. The latter is. Adults have a tendency to adopt the latter strategy when children show them paintings, drawings, models, writing, etc., without sensing the child's reason for sharing that representation with them. This can put children off sharing their products. We need to be sensitive.

Amanda (three years) draws an A on its side. She is not inviting criticism of the spatial position of the letter A. She is annoyed by such a comment, because this is her personal celebration of her name, and she is lying on her side. She wants us to share the celebration of her representation of self. As Sylvia Ashton Warner (1965) pointed out, the letters in our names are emotionally powerful, and belong to us in a special way.

Hannah at four years draws swimming pools like a 'Ha' for Hannah. Tom at 11 years melts wax candles into a large block. He then carves out the letters 'TB'. In these examples, children want admiration for their personal creations. They are not designed to be publicly scrutinised products.

We can see that the distinction between free-flow play and personal products of representation is slight. Sensitive adults can encourage, enable and act as catalysts for the development of both. Unfortunately, they can also cause both free-flow play and personal products to be stifled, to evaporate, or to go underground, through insensitivity. If these aspects of learning are arrested as they develop, this has serious implications for the child's future development. Rich free-flow play, wide ranging and free, and rich personal products in representation, are the mechanism for the rich publicly shared and scrutinised products of representation which every culture emphasises.

Adults can help, hinder or damage the development of rich representational products

(a) Hindering and damaging representation and free-flow play

The child who draws round a template, fills in an outline with colouring or screwed-up tissue paper, or who only does close observation drawings of plants, animals, etc., or only makes up a model using a kit, is not being offered experiences which lead to high-level products of representational functioning. He/she will be kept at a low level, because the message is: 'you can't do it on your own – you need guaranteed success with a template, outline or kit'. This kind of activity does not enable children to keep hold of their own experiences; it creates dependency on external props, and an attitude of 'I'm not very good at drawing', or 'How do you make an aeroplane?'. It emphasises other people's representations, rather than encouraging children to represent their own experiences. Representation of this kind is about as far away from free-flow play as you can get, fulfilling hardly any of the 12 features.

As Gardner (1982, p. 211) points out, this is serious if it is allowed to develop and take root. By the time children reach adolescence, self-criticism is developing painfully and fast, and needs a firm basis of self-confidence and success if adolescents are confidently to come through the searching scrutiny to which they subject themselves, their writing, paintings, dances, etc.

Rufus (6 years) is in a home and a school where he draws confidently. He has a new teacher, who wants the children to make Valentine cards. He draws a heart. She then shows him a template and asks him whether he wouldn't like it to be exactly shaped. Fortunately, for his future development, he says he would prefer his shape, because his Mum would like him to do it himself or it wouldn't be his any more. He goes on to draw 10 heart-shaped balloons, based on one he won at a fair. He has turned the situation so that he can use his own experience, which is what representation is about.

(b) Helping rich representational products to develop

Amandip (four years) and Sadiq (four years) brought to school their He Man dolls. Sukvinder brought her My Little Pony. It was the nursery school's policy to discourage low-level play, and the staff had to make a difficult decision whether or not to ban these toys, which seemed to encourage stereotyped, repetitive free-flow play (Gussin Paley, 1986). The play tended to be fights, or combing the mane, and was gender stereotyped. It was agreed that the teacher would use the toys as part of the props for the story of Pegasus, the flying horse in Greek mythology. The children gave their permission, and she added wings to My Little Pony. The audience was agog throughout the telling of the story, and afterwards the themes of the story, and the characters, found their way into the free-flow play and the representations of the children – e.g. Amandip painted the horse and his He Man, and wanted the painting to be put on the wall.

The teacher extended the possibilities for use of these toys in an indirect way, and gave the children ideas which they took up in their free-flow play. She was also delighted that they often wanted to make this public, and to discuss their paintings and models with her. Meadows and Cashdan (1990) also used literature, e.g. the *Watership Down* story, to encourage a wealth of ideas which children could use in their play, but the approach taken was more adult-dominated and led. In this case, the whole classroom was set up with props which took up the literary theme. The Pegasus story-telling situation was more open-ended, and the children were without pressure to take up the myth. It was simply one of many options.

When children begin to have the courage to place the products of their representation in the publicly shared domain, they need help from adults. Accepting and acting on constructive criticism is not easy to do. In the next example, we shall see that Babatunde, Chris and Nasreen were actively seeking help in doing this. They were not free-flow playing. Their products were not personal and idiosyncratic; they were opened up for public scrutiny, and the children wanted to make them better and better. These children had experienced sensitivity from adults in reaching this stage, and were constantly moving from the public domain, as in this example, to the more private domain of free-flow play, where they removed this pressure from themselves. Free-flow play helped them to make their representations all the richer.

Babatunde (seven years) pressed flowers and wanted to make greetings cards with them. A tulip went mouldy on the card. He showed it to his teacher, wondering why. Techniques were discussed and introduced, such as using less fleshy flowers, more absorbent material (blotting paper rather than kitchen paper) and a heavier pile of books.

Chris (four years) wanted to make a dough man. He wanted it to be stiff so that the eyes didn't fall off. he was grateful for help in putting it on a board on a radiator, so that it stiffened with the heat.

Nasreen (four years) made a plate of fruit from clay. She showed it to her teacher, who admired it. Germaine (four years) said, 'What's that?'. She replied that it was a strawberry. 'It doesn't look like one,' Germaine said. Nasreen said she couldn't do the 'bits' over it. The teacher found some tomatoes, and they removed and washed the pips. It wasn't ideal, but Nasreen decided to stick them on, and seemed to feel that it looked more like a strawberry. Germaine approved. Here we see a product discussed, shared and altered to the creator's satisfaction.

However, it is important to note that children need a similar approach in the way they are helped as they free-flow play. when we are invited into the home corner, we are initially there to admire, and not to scrutinise and criticise.

Adults were invited by Katie (seven years), Hannah (seven years), Raymond (six years), Charlotte (four years) and Tom (five years) to go into the museum they had made in the garage. They wanted the adults to become characters, so that everyone could free-flow play together. They played for several days off and on. However, they needed help in extending props – getting extra tables, chairs, old curtains, etc. – in order for their free-flow play to progress.

During free-flow play there is less direct discussion with adults, in comparison with the discussion of developing representational products, e.g. the clay plate of fruit made by Nasreen. Adults are there to enable the players, indirectly and sensitively, to alter and develop their free-flow play. There is no definite product, as there was for Nasreen.

Summary of representation

Free-flow play and rich representation share the same features, with the important exception that free-flow play has no products, and is a process. On the other hand, representation is both a process and a product. There is a fine distinction between free-flow play and the highly personal, idiosyncratic products that the child may not choose to share at all, or may only want to share with selected people. Initially, these are to be celebrated, rather than scrutinised. Insensitive adults hinder and damage free-flow play and representation as they develop. Sensitive adults help these aspects of learning and development to enrich each other. Rich free-flow play brings the possibility of rich representation. An adult-dominated emphasis on products undermines free-flow play, and the personal representations that are fundamental to what we call rich representation. Templates, tracing, pre-structured kits, outlines, the screwed-up tissue paper syndrome, have nothing to do with rich representation. They hinder it. They are just about as far from free-flow play as it is possible to get.

Isadora Duncan, the great dancer, said (1930, p. 30), 'I wonder how many parents realise that by the so-called education they are giving their children, they are only driving them into the commonplace, and depriving them of any chance of doing anything beautiful or original'. Parents do not want the commonplace for their children. It is therefore all the more important that teachers and nursery nurses share what they know of the importance of free-flow play in helping high standards, or rich products of representation, in education.

Decentration

In Bruce (1987), a chapter was devoted to the importance of decentration in learning and development. Seeing things from other points of view, with different feelings, through different relationships, is fundamental to free-flow play. There is no better way to step outside yourself, and to see yourself and others in a new light and with new understanding. Although the importance of decentrating pervades this book, entering into the 12 features in a variety of ways, it needs to be explicitly stated.

Nadia (four years) and Jody (five years) found a new girl, Jo (three years), in their nursery school class. She had an artificial arm. They were fascinated when she took it off at storytime, because she did not want to wear it all the time. That afternoon, they played together, and Nadia was Jo. She entered an alternative world to her own, in which she had no arms. She used all her knowledge of what arms are for, and before the afternoon was over, the girls had created an exciting and appropriate environment, and knew about Jo as they hadn't before. 'Wallowing' means looking at things from all aspects, ideas, feelings and relationships. It involves massive decentration.

Language – an aspect of representation

Spoken and written language are important ways of representing and communicating with both ourselves and others. Verbal language is the most public aspect of representation, using specific and culturally agreed sounds and symbols.

In the previous section, we looked at the non-spoken forms of representation. The importance of spoken and written language has dominated research for the last 20 years, as an inevitable outcome of the move towards 'tightening up' and making the curriculum 'more specific'. Whilst we must not neglect spoken and written words as an aspect of representation, this book seeks to put its importance into perspective. Dance, drama, painting, sculpture, music, facial expression, body language, mathematical symbols, eye contact, and touch, are all important ways of representing and communicating, and are often just as precise as spoken words.

When children and adults free-flow play, they do not have to speak, though they often do. What they say may or may not be 'heard' by those with whom they free-flow play. As Kathy Nelson demonstrates in stating an advance script, the script may or may not be taken up by others. Spoken words are important, but not vital. As Roy McConkey (1986, p. 94) stresses, children with various disabilities, including language impairment, can be helped to play, with success. Because spoken language currently dominates our understanding of development, adults do not always understand that children can free-flow play without it. Language needs action as an accompaniment, or the situation has no meaning for the child (Krashan 1981).

Conclusion

In this chapter, we have seen that the games and representations of children are linked with the culture in which they live. In different parts of the world, in different cultures, in different groups and families, free-flow play is valued, constrained or encouraged differently. The child who develops free-flow play, is also developing a powerful means of entering into games, representations, humour and decentration, at a high level of functioning. It is therefore important that all children are helped to develop free-flow play, so that they have full access, and can contribute, to their culture and beyond, with the highest quality possible.

In the next chapter, we look at Chaos Theory, which helps us further to give status to the unique contribution of free-flow play in the child's education.

7 Better Theoretical Support – Chaos Theory

Education does not operate in a vacuum

Susan Isaacs once remarked, 'I do wish we could give up teaching those dreary old theories of play' (in Gardner, 1969, p. 155). All of the theories that we looked at in Chapter 2, in their own way, value play in the broad sense. Most give free-flow play a central place in education, but all regard play as important, even if only as a means of refuelling the human system. None of the theories is perfect – but since theories are products of the human mind, that's inevitable. We have to keep searching to formulate ever better theories, which take us forward in our understanding, and in what we manage to do. It follows that as we strive to do this, we are influenced by the general philosophies of life that are dominant in our society.

The world of education therefore does not operate in a vacuum. Theory – educational, scientific, or whatever – is in a constant state of becoming. It never does become – or hopefully not. To become would mean that as educators, we had got in a rut, or jumped on a new magic method which gave the answer. In either situation, we should have stopped thinking for ourselves, and used habit or the thinking of others, rather than our own, to dominate our work with children. It is important that educators keep up with and make thoughtful connections with developments in other fields, such as science. This enables us to maintain a state of becoming, and is in essence what informed and reflective practice is about. Children need close contact with thoughtful and developing adults.

What has changed?

Philosophy has always influenced the way we relate to our universe. We saw in the last section that educational thinking is subject to the same influences as other areas of knowledge and understanding. As time has gone by, many of the issues discussed by philosophers have moved into the world of science. Until then, individuals might intuitively have sensed particular knowledge, but through science it became possible to explore, with less intuition and more certainty.

It is probably true to say that the predominant view of the universe is now a scientific rather than philosophical one. In saying this, we need to remember that a philosophical view is not the same as a religious view. There are scientists who find no conflict between religious and scientific approaches, for example. This modern world view, which has developed over the last few centuries, has gradually begun to have an impact on the way educators regard free-flow play. Until this century, free-flow play had been elusive to the scientific approach, and so had remained in the realms of philosophy for a long time. As we saw in Chapter 2, Froebel began the trend to move free-flow play from philosophy towards science.

However, the scientific thinking of Froebel's time, with its emphasis on the cosmos, influenced by the Greeks, has continued to develop – from Newtonian science, to quantum mechanics. The last 50 years have seen a new revolution in scientific theory. If we, as the modern educators of young children, are concerned to follow Froebel's lead, in taking our understanding of free-flow play beyond intuition and philosophy and into a modern scientific approach, we need to pay heed to this so that we do not use outmoded scientific approaches in studying free-flow play (Bruce, Enfield Early Years Course, November, 1990).

The nature of the change in scientific theorising

Certainty

Sir Isaac Newton, in the seventeenth century, set the scene for classical science through his laws of movement. His theories were the driving force behind the British Industrial Revolution in the late nineteenth century (Stewart, 1988, p. 1): 'Human kind slowly came to realise that nature has many regularities, which can be analysed, predicted and exploited.'

Classical science rests on the search for regularity. In previous chapters, we have seen that free-flow play is anything but a regular process in the way it presents itself.

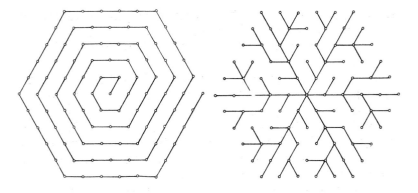

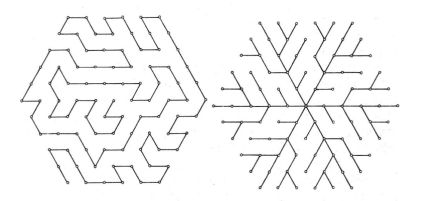

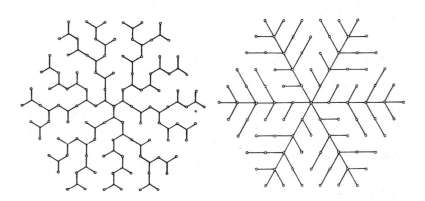

Figure 3   Some basic patterns. (Source: Patterns in Nature. *Copyright © 1974 by Peter S. Stevens.)*

It is difficult to research it through this approach. Rowland (1990, personal communication) writes:

> If you fed the starting conditions into a problem, then, when you worked it out, you would find one solution, and one solution only. The accuracy of the answer would be determined only by how accurate your starting values were, and by how well you had done your arithmetic. It was exact, one to one, a 'deterministic' outlook . . . if you knew the pressure of the steam you were supplying to the pistons of a steam train and you also knew the size of the pistons, the weight of the train etc. you would predict the rate at which it would accelerate, the amount of fuel it should use on a journey etc . . . In short, the universe was seen as a huge machine and society a sort of machine within that machine.

Galileo, watching a pendulum swing, ignored any irregularities. In the same way, Newton ignored the problems of predicting the outcome of three balls colliding simultaneously because the results were unpredictable. It was too difficult. In other words, he only developed his laws of motion in relation to certain aspects of moving objects. As Gleick (1988, p. 68) points out, 'The solvable systems are the ones shown in textbooks. They behave'. Problems that did not behave were left to one side. The same can be said of free-flow play. It does not behave, and so it does not appeal to researchers seeking out regularities, or predictable outcomes, using classical scientific methodology.

In order to tackle its irregular nature, free-flow play can either be ignored by researchers, or got rid of by transforming it into something tangible to study, i.e. changing it so that it can be pinned down as structured or guided play. It is natural to try to make order and regularity in our lives, so that we can predict, and have some definite sense of direction, and we often see this sort of behaviour in young children. The teacher asked PJ (six years) to divide into seven pieces the flapjack he had cooked in the group. He cut it into eight pieces, and pushed one piece away, saying, 'We don't need that'. PJ, like Galileo and Newton, did what he could and ignored what he couldn't.

Uncertainty

By contrast with the Victorian 'Age of Certainty' discussed in the last section, the times in which we live have been labelled 'The Age of Uncertainty'. One only has to mention the word 'environment', for example, to realise this. Just where we shall be in a few years time, with regard to changes in the planet (due to the 'greenhouse effect' of using fuels, the 'ozone effect' from industrial sprays, etc., and the effect on the environment in general from cutting down all the forests) is anybody's guess.

(a) Probability

But, as with the Victorians, our outlook is being altered by deeper philosophical changes arising in science. The seed for this was in fact sown about 100 years ago, when it began to be realised that some scientific ideas could only be expressed in terms of probability, not certainty. If you have a tiny particle of pollen floating in water, for instance, it represents such a small target that the water molecules moving in its region do not hit it evenly. Sometimes more of them hit it on one side than on the other, so it wobbles about, appearing to dance a jig. If you watch it long enough it seems to take a random walk (known to the scientific fraternity as the 'drunken sailor' effect), and you can only calculate the probability of how far it will move in a given time.

Then, 60 years ago, the realisation began to dawn that the laws that applied to ordinary things were only averages. The apparent exactness of the laws was due to the fact that when you are dealing with enormous numbers of atoms, variations in behaviour average out. Since ordinary objects do in fact consist of such enormous numbers of atoms, they exhibit this average – apparently exact – behaviour. But when you get down to the nitty-gritty of following the behaviour of individual atoms, it is found that they follow much less predictable behaviour than the laws of Newton. The science of all this is what we know as 'Quantum mechanics'. The unpredictability we have just noted it contains, is the well-known 'Heisenburg's Uncertainty Principle'.

Books are written round the Uncertainty Principle, so it is only possible to give a *very* rough sketch of it here. It means that the small particles of which matter is made, such as electrons in atoms, never keep still, but buzz around all the time in a way that makes it impossible to know exactly where they are. Imagine a fly crawling up and down the blade of an aeroplane propeller as it is whirring round. The fly could be anywhere within the area swept out by the propeller. Atoms and electrons are, of course, much tinier than propellers, but imagine the whirring fly scaled down so that it is too small to see even with a microscope. So, very roughly, an electron can be thought of as an invisible, tiny whirr. Solid matter is held together by these tiny whirrs meshing together. In some cases, the whirring electrons can hop from atom to atom and carry electricity: this is what happens when a wire conducts an electrical current. In fact, our whole knowledge of matter is now based upon this principle. It is a fascinating thought that by introducing the concept of uncertainty, we have been able to develop all the things like transistors, microchips, lasers, etc., which make the modern world what it is. Without it, there would have been no televisions, computers, video-recorders and the like. Together with this practical effect, the underlying philosophy – that a degree of unpredictability is inherent to the nature of things – has started to enter into general thought.

This approach is not yet visible in the attempts of researchers in early childhood education to take a truly scientific approach. Research on free-flow play is therefore 60 years at least behind the scientific times.

Interestingly, the very computers that quantum physics made possible, have in themselves enabled us to study systems that do not behave in a classical, regular way. One example of this is the study of 'non-linear' systems. The contrast between linear and non-linear systems can be illustrated by the burning of gunpowder. If the gunpowder is in the form of a fuse, burning is smooth and regular, and the length of fuse burnt is proportional to the time – twice as much burns in two minutes as in one minute. But if you cram the powder into a bomb-case, the first bit that burns increases the temperature and pressure of the rest, which therefore burns faster, and the reaction soon becomes explosive. Systems where the rate at which something changes is dependent on the amount of change that has already taken place are called 'non-linear'. A growing child is non-linear in development, especially with regard to mental development and free-flow play as an aspect of this. Boden (p. 150) cites Piaget's outline of developmental stages as an example of non-linear development, 'emerging through a dialetical interaction with the child's world'.

Non-linear systems often exhibit 'deterministic chaos', which is dealt with in the next section.

(b) Deterministic chaos

Thought is now moving a step further. The Quantum Theory simply regarded the Uncertainty Principle as something that must be accepted as a fact of life. Uncertainty was built into it. But increasingly over the last century, an even more startling theory has emerged – where uncertainty is not deliberately built in, but arises even in calculations that are theoretically exact. This is 'Chaos Theory'. It is a theory of mathematics which says that there will be many situations where you can predict the behaviour of a system exactly, *but* only if you know the starting conditions with an accuracy that can never be achieved in our universe. This sounds like a theory which could make a valuable contribution to our study of free-flow play.

The classic system of this sort is the weather. In the computer programs which are used to predict this, tiny variations in the data fed in (temperatures, wind speeds and the positions where they were measured) can result in enormous, unpredictable variations in the results. Put another way round, a tiny disturbance in the weather in one part of the world, caused by nothing more than the beat of a butterfly's wing, may, many days later, start a hurricane on the other side of the world. This is known aptly as the 'butterfly effect'. It might be argued that the disturbance could nevertheless have been measured with the required accuracy, but that in fact would be impossible. To state those positions, the computer would have to work to so many decimal places that the size of its memory chips would occupy the whole universe – a logical impossibility. In other words, unpredictability is unavoidable.

However, this is not total. We all know that it is possible to make short-term weather forecasts with a fair chance of being right. But the longer the time for which you are forecasting ahead, the less accurate they become. If you want to get hands-on experience of a system that obeys Chaos Theory, try the Medieval Water Torture: the kitchen tap will illustrate it. An excellent account of this, and of other aspects of Chaos Theory, is given in *Does God Play Dice?* by Ian Stewart, but the book is rather mathematical, so I'll summarise. Your tap may behave differently from mine – remember, we are dealing with unpredictability.

Get the tap just running with a thin continuous stream, then throttle it back very gently until the stream breaks into drops. If they fall with a regular rhythm, throttle back a bit more. In this way you should find a region where the regular beat breaks up. There may be a rush of drops, then a pause; then another rush, but to a different rhythm – and so on. This illustrates another aspect of Chaos Theory – apparent regularity ('quasi-regularity'), where events seem to behave in a regular way, but not quite. The system never repeats itself exactly. (This was where the ancient torture came in when the drops fell on the victims forehead. One can adapt to regular drips, but waiting for one that should come – but doesn't – then does unexpectedly . . .)

Figure 4   An instantaneous photograph of a 'splash of milk'.
(Copyright © 1957, Estate of Harold E. Edgerton, Courtesy of Palm Press, Inc.)

The tap can be used to illustrate another property of Chaos Theory. Sometimes the system behaves fairly regularly, sometimes it doesn't. Put a cup or tumbler in the sink and allow it to fill from the tap. Now turn the tap off and then open it step-by-step, observing both the falling stream and the surface of the water in the cup at each stage. Because the results differ from tap to tap, I cannot say exactly what will happen, but you will *probably* go through some stages where the drips are almost perfectly regular, and others where they are not. At higher flows, the water may form a solid-looking, smooth, regular column, but a bit further on, the column may oscillate in shape. The fact that a 'chaotic' system may sometimes behave regularly explains why Newtonian science was able to treat some parts of the Universe as if regularity ruled. By trial and error, the early scientists had locked onto the parts that did behave in this way. Wisely at the time, they ignored systems (such as three balls colliding simultaneously) where their equations could not be applied. They should not be disparaged for this. In so doing, they set up the knowledge which allows us to progress from their world view to the present.

Another familiar system that is believed to come under the theory is the beating of the heart. Even when a person is at rest, this is rarely exactly regular, though it is nearly so.

(c) Chaos theory: a theory of everyday life

In fact, it is now thought that most of the systems we encounter in daily life are subject to Chaos Theory. Here are a few:

(1) The flow of water in rivers and pipes when it flows fast and becomes turbulent.

(2) World economic cycles – where trade flourishes, then recedes, then booms again in ways that are difficult to predict.

(3) Flu epidemics.

(4) The number of ladybirds in the garden. They eat greenfly until there are not enough left for them. So the ladybirds die back. So then the greenfly get ahead, which means the ladybirds can get ahead, and so on. (But not in an exactly regular way.)

(5) Free-flow play. The human body consists of a mass of linked chemical reactions. The food we eat does not appear in the muscles and brain as, say, bread and butter, but is broken down and turned into one different substance after another by a series of linked chemcial reactions. It has been found that linked chemical reactions of a similar sort are subject to Chaos Theory. In view of this, the wide differences between the way different peoples' bodies work are therefore not surprising, and, of course, human bodies and other organisms do not just come into existence fully formed. They have to grow from small seeds. It is probably simplest to consider something like a tree. Here, a branch divides into, say, two; each of which divides again to give a total of four, and so on. It has been found that there is a whole new type of mathematics ('fractals'), which describe such processes. Jonathan Swift expresses this,

> Little fleas have on their backs
> Little fleas to bite 'em
> And smaller fleas have lesser fleas
> And so – *ad infinitum.*

Fractals constitute the science of things where pattern at a large level – say, branches – is repeated at a smaller level – say, twigs. And at even smaller levels – for example, the veins in the leaves. The pattern is not followed absolutely rigidly at all stages, but contains variations. This fits with the fact that fractals have been found to be closely related to Chaos Theory. The growth of a human body is much more complex than this, of course, but it does consist of a process where one group of cells is laid down and this, in turn, gives rise to another group, and so on. All this is carried out by linked chemical reactions.

An important aspect of this is that humans will have built into their development aspects of Chaos Theory. That is to say, there will be order in their behaviour, but it will not be rigid order. There will be irregularities, varying from the slight to the catastrophic. This is, after all, completely in accord with people as we know them. So the paradigm has changed. We are in the age of the 'chaotic' or self-developing child, as opposed to the Victorian view of the 'cogwheel child'.

We need to re-consider what it is to take a scientific and rigorous approach to the study of free-flow play in educational research. Searching for regularities, the tendency to date is unlikely to help our knowledge and understanding of free-flow play to progress. Instead, we need to address the issues of methodology raised through the deterministic uncertainty of Chaos Theory. It may be that the deterministic aspects of free-flow rest in the 12 features of the process itself.

Important influences on the development of chaos theory

Henri Poincaré and his maps (The 1880s)

Poincaré was born in 1854, two years after Froebel died. He was a mathematician who believed that shape and motion

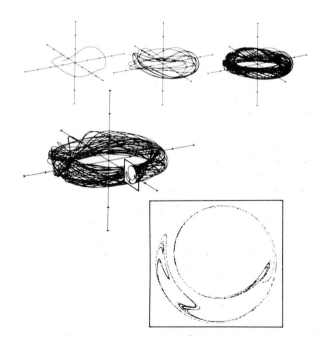

Figure 5   The chaotic behaviour of a pendulum swinging, and a child free-flow playing demonstrate irregularity in the universe. (Source: Chaos *by J. Gleik.)*

were really different aspects of the same thing. He used shapes (his maps) to show how whole systems behaved, and developed topology.

Topology is the study of the shapes of pathways in space: for instance, the path of the earth around the sun. Though this might seem to be fixed, it does change slowly over the centuries, due to the gravitational pull of the other planets. It will never repeat itself exactly within the lifetime of the universe. Poincaré was, as Gleick (1988) says, 'a unifier, a seeker of general principles'.

It is interesting to note that in this century, Jean Piaget, through his concept of schemas, emphasises configurative and dynamic aspects of behaviour, i.e. both the static shape and the moving form. In his theory, schemas are patterns of behaviour which the child repeats and generalises. Later in the chapter, we shall see that there may be useful links to be made between Piagetian schemas and Chaos Theory, as Poincaré's emphasis suggests. These have implications for free-flow play.

D'Arcy Thompson (1930s)

This biologist has won the affection and respect of many scientists. His classic book, *On Growth and Form* is a meticulous study of the universals of form and motion in nature. In this sense, it echoes the concerns of Poincaré and opens the way for Piaget's influence. D'Arcy Thompson shows a fascination with the ways that form and motion combine to make unique variations. His line of thought and research was idiosyncratic. He was a 'one-off', who made scientists think.

> The beauty of a snow crystal depends on its mathematical regularity and symmetry; but somehow the association of many variants of a single type, all related but no two the same, vastly increases our pleasure and admiration (Thompson, 1961, p. 154).

If we substitute 'the 12 underlying features of a child's free-flow play' for 'a snow crystal', we have a good example of how free-flow play can be regarded as combining shape with motion – as Poincaré, D'Arcy Thompson and Piaget imply.

*Figure 6   A snowflake growing in a snowstorm and a child free-
flow playing have much in common; they are both chaotic
systems. (Source: Chaos by J. Gleik.)*

Edward Lorenz and the 'butterfly effect' (1950s)

Sometimes things escape notice because they are in the
wrong place. Lorenz, a mathematician who became a
meteorologist because of the outbreak of World War II,
published a crucial mathematical paper in 1963. It was not
published in a mathematical journal, but in the *Journal of
the Atmospheric Sciences* (Vol. 20, p. 130, 'Deterministic
Non Periodic Flow'). In effect, this was equivalent to
publishing it in *Child Education*, because it was 10 years
before it was read by a mathematician who could make
sense of it. It revealed the 'fine structure hidden within a
disorderly stream of data' (Gleick, 1988, p. 29).

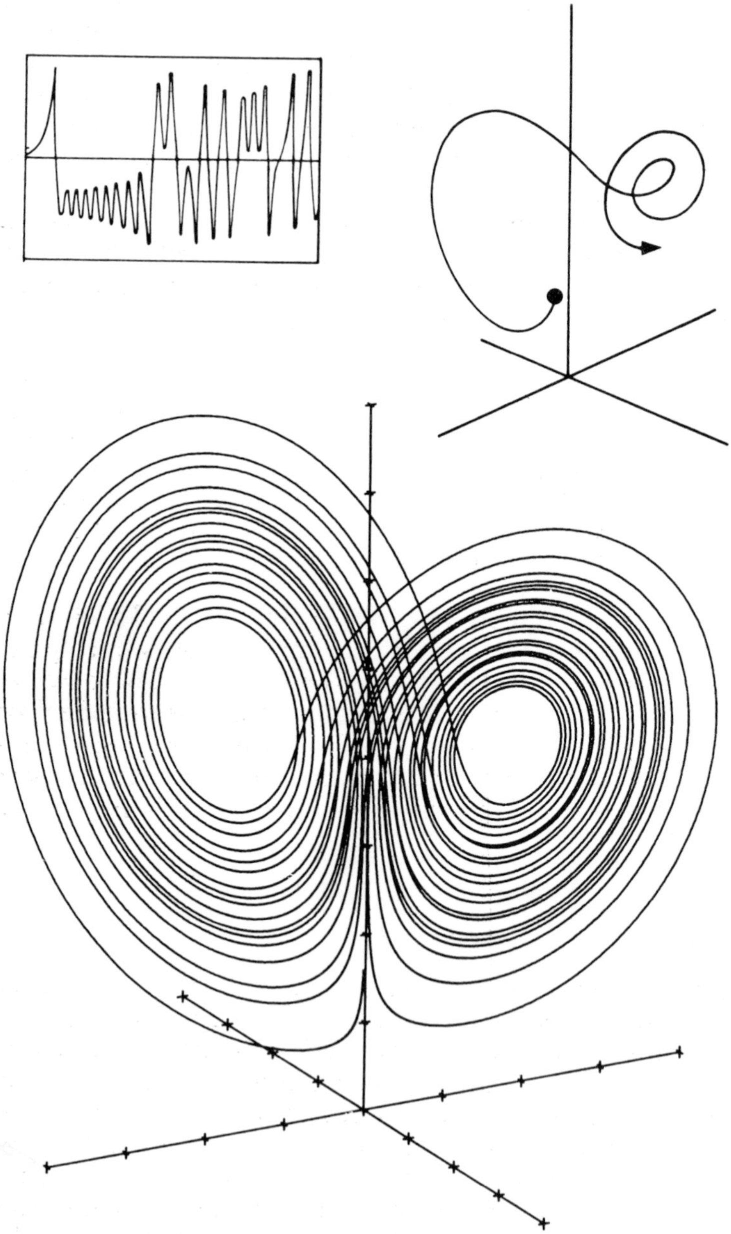

Figure 7   The way the 'butterfly effect' shows on a computer
screen has become the emblem of Chaos Theory. (Source: Chaos
by J. Gleik.)

Lorenz was fascinated by systems that never found a steady state, like the weather (or free-flow play). His 'butterfly effect', described in the previous section, was a way of seeing 'order masquerading as randomness' (Gleick, 1988, p. 22). The way the butterfly effect shows on a computer screen has become the emblem of Chaos Theory Rough-and-tumble free-flow play is a fine example. Home-corner play is another.

As those working with young children know, the arrival of a new child in the home corner can totally change the free-flow play. Vivian Gussin Paley (1986, p. 84) unwittingly describes this butterfly effect vividly.

> Christopher does try to enter the ongoing play, now that he realises it is play, but his syncopation is off. I would gladly teach him the method, if I could, but my rhythms don't work either. He must watch the children, find his own style, and practice a great deal. One thing I can do for Christopher is to stop jumping in so quickly. By substituting my own cadence too often, I may be delaying his adaptation to the rhythm, of the group.

Lorenz helped scientists to develop a whole view of systems or processes, rather than only seeing isolated parts. In order to understand the rhythms of free-flow play, we need to see the process as a whole. Using the methodology of Chaos Theory may help us to do this. We need to see both shape and movement, both form and growth, both configurations and dynamic patterns, as children free-flow play.

Mandelbrot and fractals (1960s)

Benoit Mandelbrot has been described by Gleick as an 'academic nomad', who accidentally strayed into special-isations that were not mathematics, where he started. In doing so, he made a great contribution to Chaos Theory during the 1960s, and to its development beyond mathematics. He looked at patterns which held across different scales, and found that cotton price data, when sifted through a computer, seemed random and unpredictable from the point of view of normal distribution. But when he compared daily prices of cotton with monthly prices, the changes matched perfectly. He found that 'the degree of variation had remained constant over a tumultuous 60-year period that saw two World Wars and a depression' (Gleick, 1988, p. 86). This helped him to develop his fascination for the phenomenon of scaling, which are called 'fractuals'. The example of trees, branches and twigs was given earlier in the chapter.

It may well be that free-flow play is a chaotic process, in which patterns hold across different scales. We need more data of the sort that would help us to explore this.

Peter Stevens (1970s)

D'Arcy Thompson's work was admired by a group of physicists – the 'philomorphs', at Harvard. Peter Stevens wrote up the discussions of the group in *Patterns in Nature*. This book implicitly embraces Chaos Theory, and leads us into the 1980s.

Peter Stevens and the philomorphs explore phenomena such as bubbles, tree growth, stress in bones and crab shells, rivers and meandering. They demonstrate the unifying patterns which generalise and adapt to situations, but only in so far as they are able to do so. Stevens (1976, p. 222) writes:

> The rules of nature in tree growth are rigorous, but within those rules variety abounds, and the rules show through the variations to portray a relatedness of parts that is aesthetically pleasing and a constancy of purpose that provides an external model for all human creations.

The same may be said of free-flow play. The underlying deterministic rules are expressed through the 12 features. Within these, the possibilities are endless in variation – unpredictable and uncertain.

Jean Piaget

Every so often, something stirs deep inside us. Paul Davies (1990, p.51) suggests that studying Chaos Theory has 'revealed how it is possible to reconcile the complexity of a physical world displaying haphazard and capricious behaviour with the order and simplicity of the underlying laws of nature'. That could send a prickle down our spines. Jean Pierre Petit (in Stewart, 1989, p. 146) describes it thus: 'I'VE UNDERSTOOD IT. Well, that is . . . I'm not sure exactly WHAT I've understood, but I have the impression I've understood SOMETHING'. We need to find a link from Chaos Theory, which is couched in terms appropriate for mathematicians and scientists, to the terminology relevant to those of us working with young children.

Perhaps the most discussed theory during the 1970s and 1980s for early childhood educators has been that of Jean Piaget. His influence on education has been, and remains, great; through recent extension and modification of his original theory, rather that the theory in its original state. As Margaret Boden (1979, p. 149) says, this influence 'depends less on what he said than on what he was generally believed to have said, and not at all on whether what he said was right'.

For example, she points out that many educational programmes have been inspired by Piaget. Examples would be High/Scope, or Chris Athey's 1990 Nursery Project, Constance Kamii (1973) Lavatelli (1968), but each may differ drastically in the way that his theory is interpreted. Whichever way we look at it, his work has been seminal, because 'someone has to make the conjecture before anyone can provide the refutation' (Boden, p. 153).

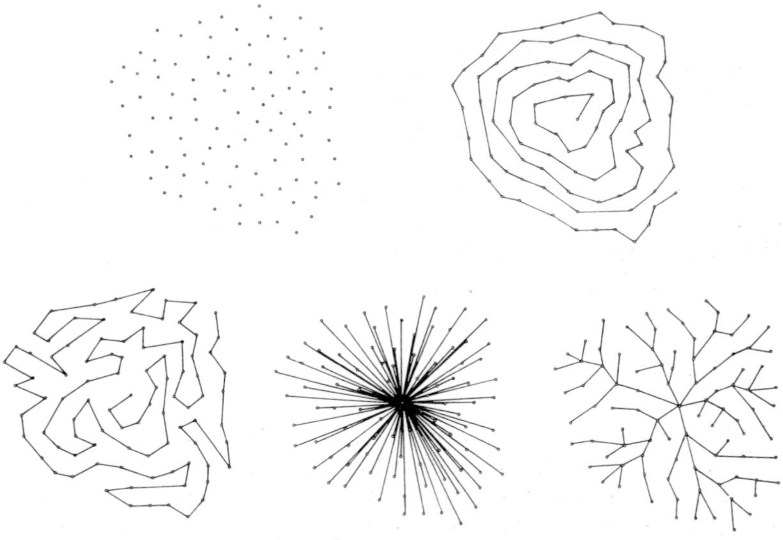

Figure 8   Movement and form are different aspects of the same thing. They make order out of apparent randomness and complexity. (Source: Patterns in Nature. *Copyright © 1974 by Peter S. Stevens.)*

Piaget, like Poincaré and D'Arcy Thompson before him, sees movement and form as different aspects of the same thing, which serve to unify randomness and complexity into order.

For Piaget, the schema is a way of unifying and creating general principles, which operate to give a basic underlying structure to the processes of children's behaviour. Boden (p. 154) praises this aspect of his theory, with its 'stress on self-organising mental structures and cognitive trans-formations'. A schema is a repeatable pattern of organis-ational behaviour which the child generalises, e.g. the trajectory (banging, jumping, climbing up and down, throwing, etc.). Schemas help us to see the order behind apparent disorder in children's behaviour (Athey, 1990; Nutbrown, 1989; Matthews, 1988; Bruce, 1987; Nicolls, 1986). They operate in configurative (static) and dynamic (moving) forms. They operate at different levels (sensori-motor, symbolic), and with functional dependencies (as in cause and effect).

As we have seen, chaotic systems do not behave regularly. The Piagetian schema may offer us ways to study the deterministic elements in free-flow play. It may help us to tackle what seems to be random and complex in a way that seeks to see the process as a whole, rather than in isolated parts. We see that apparently, 'lawless behaviour is governed entirely by law' (Stewart, 1989, p. 155).

For example, Katie (two years) and Hannah (two and a half years) were in the paddling pool. Hannah kept tipping water over Katie's head with a cup. Katie disliked it. The play was stopped by adults. The next day, the girls were again in the paddling pool. Hannah suggested that they play hair washing. Adults became a little worried, but she pulled back Katie's head and tipped water over her hair – though not over her face, as her mother did when washing her hair. This time, Katie enjoyed the game, and wanted to do the same to Hannah, who agreed. The play was imaginative and sustained, and represented a leap forward since the previous day. It was unpredictable, but there was an underlying order in the transporting of water from pool to cup to head.

Tom (three years) is on the shingle beach. He picks up pebbles, and makes a row. He remembers his mother has a fat felt pen in her bag, and asks for it. He draws a circle on each pebble, and says, 'These are monsters'. He makes them growl, and moves them about. He doesn't want other children to touch them. He talks to himself about what the monsters are doing. No-one could have predicted that he would play with the pebbles in this way. However, an observer of Tom over several weeks, such as his mother, would have been able to note his fascination with circles, enclosures and spheres. This is evident in this piece of free-flow play.

In these two examples, we have seen the free-flow play being 'governed by law', in the form of the transporting schema and the enclosure schema. Gleick describes a similar process (1988, p. 311) in nature.

> As a growing snowflake falls to earth, typically floating in the wind for an hour or more, the choices made by the branching tips at any instant depend sensitively on such things as the temperature, the humidity and the presence of impurities in the atmosphere. The six tips of a single snowflake, spreading within a millimetre space, feel the same temperatures, and because the laws of growth are purely deterministic, they maintain a near perfect symmetry. But the nature of turbulent air is such that any pair of snowflakes will experience very different paths. The final flake records the history of all the changing weather conditions it has experienced, and the combinations may as well be infinite.

A child's free-flow play is also unique, but unlike the snowflake, it is also expressive of that child's personality, as well as his/her experiences.

Through this aspect of Piaget's theory, he may have left us a precious legacy through which to begin exploring the patterns, scales, apparent randomness and complexity of free-flow play in education. It may help us to establish the deterministic structure within the system of free-flow play, and to see it as a whole, rather than concentrating on the outcomes of free-flow play. It may help us to justify free-flow play as a process important in its own right. It may help us to seek out the non-linear aspects of development – the jagged edges and sudden leaps (Gleick, 1988, p. 5) – rather than to avoid them, studying only the neat and tidy aspects of learning and development.

Most people, when they study Piaget, look at his contribution to identifying what is regular and certain in a child's development, e.g. his much debated Stage Theory. Perhaps it is time to turn to the aspects of his theory which lead us to find chaos, and a new kind of order (Stewart).

Chaos: A new kind of order in free-flow play

In this chapter, we have looked at the thinking of Poincaré, D'Arcy Thompson, Lorenz, Mandelbrot, the Harvard philo-morphs and Piaget. They all present what Gleick (1988, p. 5) calls 'certain sensibilities', which he regards as necessary for the understanding of chaotic systems such as free-flow play. These are as follows.

1 An eye for pattern, especially pattern that appears on different scales at the same time.

2 Fascination with what appears to be random or complex.

3 Interest in determinism and its nature.

4 Searching for the whole, rather than exploring isolated parts – such as the single types of cells in the human body, or single chemical substances in foods (a good wine might contain 200 substances), etc.

5 Interest in the process of becoming, rather than being.

6 Focus on non-linear systems.

7 Emphasis on areas most people leave out, in order to get 'a good, simple understanding' (Gleick, 1988, p. 24).

How does chaos theory help us to study free-flow play?

The relationship between process and product

We have seen that, rather than focus on the products or outcomes of free-flow play (of which there are endless possibilities and variations), it is probably more useful to try to explore the underlying features which determine the process as a whole.

Gathering real data

The influence of the Greeks on science led to the study of the cosmos and our relationship with it. Chaos Theory is helping us to get our feet on the ground, so that we can look at the science of everyday life (Stewart, 1989, p. 43).

> Mathematicians who can calculate the motion of a satellite of Jupiter are beginning to puzzle about the motion of a snowflake in a blizzard.

As we saw, in previous sections, the data we need to collect will be different. For example, the ecologist Schaffer thought he had found patterns in the breeding habits of bees on the Arizona mountains. However, after a few summers, the patterns disintegrated and it all seemed random. He was very dispirited. Luckily, he attended a lecture on chaology in 1980, by the chemist Harry Swinney. He showed Swinney his data, and by using computers they discovered the typical underlying deterministic patterns of a chaotic system. Swinney described Schaffer's data as 'real data', and it is the gathering of 'real data' that is urgently needed in early childhood education.

Studies which have attempted to gather continuous and formative observations over time, rather than short, sharp observations, are more likely to yield 'real data'. Examples would be Isaacs (1930s), Eng (1930s), Navarra (1957), Weir (1970s), Gussin Paley (1980s), Matthews (1988), Athey (1990), Gura (ed., directed by Bruce, in press, 1992). There is a tendency overall to seek out neat and tidy methods, but 'real data' is not of this nature. Reducing free-flow play to a regular system, with specific inputs and specific, measurable outputs – as in classical science – is not helpful. Paul Davies (1990) would describe it as 'idealised fiction'. The study of free-flow play represents a great challenge for research. We need to understand it better in order to maintain its central place in education, and indeed life. As Richard Feynman, the Nobel Prize-winning physicist said, 'The thing that doesn't fit is the most interesting'.

Because something does not easily fit current and obsolete research methods, it does not mean that it is not important. That is why we urgently need to learn how to gather the 'real data', to enable us to link with modern science, and to explore the underlying deterministic rules of uncertainty, as in free-flow play.

The way forward

Chaology gives theoretical support to the study of free-flow play in ways that give it high status and a central place in education. Chaos Theory helps us to look at existing theories of play with a new perspective. This leads us to two ways forward.

1 Early childhood educators need to link with modern science, and to seek advice on methods of collecting 'real data' through which to study free-flow play. This will involve long-term, continuous studies of children, rather than dipstick, summative approaches. After all, Swinney the chemist and Schaffer the ecologist made a powerful combination in using continuously gathered data.

2 We need to become involved in the kind of classroom-based research which helps us to collect 'real data' (McAuley, 1990, p. 87).

Those working directly and continuously with children, in home, care or educational settings, are in a powerful position to gather such data. This presents an important argument for having a high adult/child ratio, which would enable such developments. It also means that adults must be good observers of children, and be helped towards being this by staff who are highly trained catalysts in the data gathering process. When parents, nursery nurses, teachers and researchers work together in this way, there is the possibility of exciting developments in our understanding of free-flow play as an integrating mechanism in the education of the child, and probably, as the Singers (1990) suggest, important for adults too – although the form of free-flow play will change as we grow older.

An approach that might give indications of fruitful ways in which to proceed is that used in the study of chimpanzee groups by Jane Goodall (1990). Chimpanzees are the closest relatives to human beings, and the essential hereditary chemical in their systems (the substance DNA, which determines whether you will be a frog, a tree or a human, for example) differs from ours by less than 2 per cent. In the early days of Goodall's pioneering work, when she attributed mind-processes to the chimpanzees similar to those that occur in humans (and particularly in children), scientists brought up in the 'classical' tradition were inclined to disapprove of her methods. However, these methods have proved resoundingly successful and her work is now held in high regard, having led to entirely new discoveries. For example, she has discovered that – contrary to previous opinion, derived from 'classical' laboratory studies of chimps – groups of chimpanzees in their natural state will wage war on each other and will resort to quite sophisticated strategies to do so. It is necessary to read Goodall's books to get a full picture of the way in which she works, but the essence is that the subject must be studied in the everyday setting, and the whole behaviour noted – not just that which conforms to regular patterns.

Perhaps Jane Goodall herself – introducing her book (1990) on the years of continuous study she has made of chimpanzees, a species under threat – should sum up this chapter. The issues are the same as those facing the future of the central place of free-flow play in education.

Only if we understand, can we care
Only if we care, will we help
Only if we help, shall they be saved.

8 Practical Strategies

In this chapter, we look at three major strategies which encourage rich free-flow play to develop. These are:

1 Good observation and recording of children's free-flow play.

2 Supporting the child's free-flow play through a familiar context and through firsthand experience, which give opportunities and access to free-flow play.

3 Extending the child's experiences, using the familiar to introduce the unfamiliar.

We can summarise this as the need to observe, support and extend the child's free-flow play. It is a useful strategy in any early childhood education setting.

1 Observing the child's free-flow play

Enjoying our work with children

Observing and recording children's free-flow play should not be made a burden. Unless we enjoy our contact with children, we shall not be able to bear all the stresses and physical exhaustion which seem to be part of any caring profession.

It is particularly difficult for teachers working in reception classes full of four year olds. Report after report (Osborn and Milbank, 1987; Clark, 1988; NFER, 1989; All Party Select Committee Report on Provision for Under Fives, 1989; HMI Survey of Reception Classes, 1989; Pascal, 1990, Rumbold Committee Report, 1990) suggests that this practice is to be condemned, and that children under five need a maximum adult/child ratio of 1:13. Teachers struggling to work with a 1:30 ratio in a class of four year olds cannot be blamed for achieving less observation and recording of children's free-flow play or of any other aspect of their education. In other words, we can only manage what is humanly possible during a day, even if we give of our best – which the vast majority of teachers do.

Observing little but often, or more and seldom

The current tendency is towards the former, in spirit; and increasingly, in practice. This is moving away from the traditions of early years practice, which favoured making lengthy chunks of observations (e.g. Isaacs). It takes some courage to observe less frequently, but for longer and in more depth, especially in the current climate of account-ability through the National Curriculum. It takes time to observe. However, the benefit is that depth of observation brings with it a greater breadth of insight into the child's free-flow play, and also into any aspect of learning and development. Teachers in the Froebel Nursery Project (Athey, 1990), and in the recent Block Play Project (Gura, ed., in press, 1992, directed by Bruce), began to see this with at first shock, and then delight and deep inner satisfaction.

Adults tend to flit from area to area, in an attempt to keep an overview and to give every child attention. This is in an attempt not to neglect any child or area. In reality, this leads to some areas being visited more frequently (e.g. junk modelling), and some children gaining more of the teacher's attention than others. If, on the other hand, we decide to be somewhere for a length of time, we are more likely to take real note of what is happening, simply because we are there long enough to pause and take stock. In fact, this eases the burdensome pressures of observation and recording. It helps us to focus in more depth (and therefore in breadth) on what children know and are learning, rather than constantly worrying about what they don't know, but need to know.

Below are some strategies for observing and recording children's free-flow play. They will work in situations with practical constraints, such as too few adults, and too many children.

Too few adults

1   Use opportunities such as tidying, or servicing an area, to observe free-flow play.

2   Keep in mind the 12 features of free-flow play, and use them as a framework to distinguish between firsthand experience and free-flow play, and between represent-ation, games and free-flow play.

(a) Remember that firsthand experience differs in that it directly gives children opportunities to wallow in ideas, feelings and relationships, and that it gives them direct experiences through which to develop skills and competence. In contrast, free-flow play is when they use the wealth of experiences we have previously offered, and when they actually apply the skills and competencies they have developed earlier through firsthand experience.

In other words, it is Features 5, 6 and 8 which distinguish firsthand experience from free-flow play.

(b) Remember that representation differs from free-flow play only in the fact that representation has products (idiosyncratic and personal, or public and shareable). Free-flow play does not have products, although it may use representations as props. In other words, it is Feature 1 which distinguishes representation and free-flow play.

(c) Remember that games differ from free-flow play only in that they have rules that are sensitive to external pressure on the child. These can be developed and negotiated between children or adults. In free-flow play, the rules are personal and idiosyncratic, lasting only whilst the play lasts. In other words, it is Feature 3 which distinguishes games from free-flow play. The more we can distinguish (probably inaccurately at times) between free-flow play and other aspects of learning and developing, the more we see its value. One of the problems in observing and recording free-flow play is understanding how it relates to other areas. We need to see it in perspective, as part of the whole curriculum.

3 Jot down dated notes on a separate card (or half a page of A4), using the 12 features as a framework, and place it in a boxfile containing a section for each child. Often, the free-flow play will involve several children, so simply file the observations under one child and make a short cross-reference under the other names – or place a photocopy under each child's name.

In an earlier chapter, we saw how the teacher was helping children to tidy up the home corner, but was in a strong position whilst doing so to both encourage and observe the children's free-flow play. The burglar play developed, where the children pretended to be policemen chasing burglars. Awareness of the 12 features would mean that during five minutes at the end of the day, the adult could jot down important observations about the children's free-flow play.

No-one has made the children play burglars; they have simply taken up an idea tossed out by the adult. The rules developed are idiosyncratic and internal to this free-flow play. They involve frequently going back to the home corner, and shouting 'nee naw' when rushing about outside. They have created an 'as if' situation, involving seeking and trying to catch, with a theme and characters. They are using what they know of chasing, searching, police, baddies, and reflecting on all of this as they wallow and make use of firsthand experiences, e.g. how hard it is to catch someone you chase, that police chases involve roaring through traffic, and that burglars make a mess. The play was sustained (20 minutes), and although none of these children had directly experienced being burgled, or being in a police chase, it helped them to consider what is involved, using their own experiences to do so. This was not representation, because although props were used (scarves as face masks), nothing lasted. It was mainly process. They were able to control their dodging about at speed, without bumping into people when outside. They helped to tidy up the home corner with equal competence, i.e. gross and fine motor skills were evident. The play was initiated by the adult, and developed into free-flow play – with personal and shared agendas being negotiated. It brought together their limited knowledge and understanding of burglary, and of being bad.

Those working with young children, through their training and their experience, often acquire impressive intuitive observational skills. Here, in a short-staffed setting, with the practical constraint of needing to encourage tidying up, the adult noted significant features in the free-flow play of several children. Over a cup of tea at the end of the day, they were recorded and placed in the box file.

In the following situation, the adult was servicing an area by checking on the safety of the children using large blocks, and found them free-flow playing a ski slope. Again, using five minutes, this was recorded through the 12 features. A card in a box file could give invaluable information on not only one child's, but several children's, free-flow play. Photocopies mean cards can be inserted for each child involved, or a cross-reference can be used. It is likely to indicate how children are taking up and using firsthand experiences that are offered, and how much use of representation is mingling with their free-flow play.

Too many children

Depending on the practical arrangements, there may be as many as 120 children (60 morning and 60 afternoon) in an open-plan setting during each day. It is not possible to observe every child as frequently as is desirable. Again, we must develop strategies to deal with these practical constraints.

(a) We need to target our observations

We need to be sure we do not over-observe some children and under-observe others. We need to target our observations. In the open-plan nursery, two children were observed by the whole team (two teachers, three nursery nurses) in the morning and two children in the afternoon. This means that each child was closely observed every six weeks, i.e. twice a term. At the end of the morning and afternoon, observations were pooled, put on cards and placed in a box file with a section for each child. Obviously the children were not observed constantly, for classroom life does not usually allow this. Children are sick, wet themselves, need help with activities, and require direct teaching, as well as indirect approaches. However, during the two and a half hours of the sessions, observations could be managed in sufficient detail so as to make the pooling of information for recording fascinating and useful. Staff were reassured to find similar observations to their own being made, or to hear about strengths they had not thought a child had. Areas avoided by particular children were also useful to know about. In both settings, parents were introduced to this way of observing children at study groups, and helped to gather observations at home.

Staff either remembered details from their observations, or jotted them down on scraps of paper whilst they observed. The reality was that in a busy classroom, it was often asking too much for them to take notes, and memory prevailed. In Redford House Nursery and Pen Green Family Centre, staff have recently joined together through inservice work, to consider ways of developing easier practical approaches to making longer chunks of observation possible. The Piagetian schema has been helpful in establishing what John Matthews calls the 'internal programme' of the child's free-flow play. In the Pen Green setting, staff focused upon friendships during free-flow play (Cathy Arnold, 1990).

Video and photography are invaluable additions to pencil and paper recording. In these two nurseries, attempts have been made to coordinate video, photographic and written records, and to share them with parents. The team approach eases the burden of feeling that record keeping 'all depends on me'.

(b) Sharing our observations

We can observe alone if we have to, or, where possible, we can use the strength of a team approach. We also need to meet regularly to share these observations, perhaps at weekly staff meetings. Again, it may not be possible to discuss 20 children's free-flow play, but if children are placed in groups with their own key workers, one child's free-flow play from each group could be discussed. This would mean looking at five children in depth each week, but every child would be known in reasonable depth by at least their own adult key worker.

(c) Tuning into the child

At the beginning of the term, staff can look at last term's records, to refresh their memories quickly of where children are in their free-flow play. When children move to new schools, records are important in helping receiving staff to tune into the children.

Children need to take part in looking at their own progress in free-flow play, as part of the reflective, metacognitive process. Primary and nursery schools are beginning to develop these. For example, at Danebury Primary School, children and adults together make books in which photographs, drawings and descriptions of free-flow play are included. These records of achievement accompany the children through the education system, and into later work settings. They are more sophisticated versions of the traditional Baby Books, which many parents keep from birth, and which bring much reflection on development and progress within the family setting in an informal, but powerful, way. However, whereas parents decide what shall be included in these, the child controls the decision-making with his/her record of achievement. So that free-flow play has a central place in these records, adults scribe what the children tell them about the play.

We know from studies (Karrby, 1988; Ditchburn, 1989) that children realise the value of free-flow play. The record of achievement means that adults are seen by the child to give free-flow play high status. However, it is important not to force children to talk about free-flow play unless they want to do so. Photographs give non-verbal status to free-flow play, and children might well be encouraged to talk spontaneously if these are selected for inclusion. The child will do this in partnership with the adult. The non-verbal is as important as the verbal.

Children can then share these records with their families, as well as with the staff who work directly with them.

(d) Parents and staff sharing records

Gina Houston, former head of a nursery school, regularly invited parents to join staff meetings targeting their children. By keeping indepth records of free-flow play, we signal to parents that we value it deeply. Throughout the book, it has been stressed that unless we establish with parents shared meanings about the importance of free-flow play, it is likely to be regarded by them as recreation from 'real work'. Given that free-flow play is central in the young child's education, this would be damaging to the child's future. All work and no free-flow play makes for dull adults. No parent wants their child to become dull.

(e) Targeting an area

Using the moment as it arrives, whilst tidying or checking an area's safe functioning, gives us finger-in-the-dyke strategies. We are forced by circumstances to indulge frequently in these.

A more premeditated strategy is to decide to be in an area, e.g. the home corner. The teachers and nursery nurses in the Froebel Block Play Project (ed., Gura, in press, 1991) found this was essential, or free-flow play with blocks was constrained and under-developed. This requires planning in advance.

Sometimes it seems as if everything is conspiring to keep us away from the area we have targeted. A child is sick, a parent needs attention, a health visitor needs to talk urgently. But once we are there, Gordon Wells (1986), suggests that we need to take what children do and say seriously. We need to try to understand what children mean. We need to act on what we think children mean.

For example, Hans (six years) and Raoul (seven years) are using the miniature farm. Hans puts the cows in a row in a field. Raoul scatters the cows. 'Not like that, silly,' Hans says, 'it's like the telly' – an advertisement where the cows dance in a line. Hans has not seen cows in a field. He is using what he has seen, which is advertisements on television. The teacher needs to know this in planning what is appropriate for Hans, or for Raoul, who has seen cows in a real field. The two boys have different needs.

When Gordon Wells (1987) talks about children as meaning makers, he emphasises the active nature of the child's learning, and the adult's need to tune into this. When Bruner (1990) talks about 'Acts of Meaning' he talks about adults helping children to make meaning of their culture. The emphasis is more on how the adult can best lead the child.

The differences between these two approaches are subtle, but important. When we see Hans and Raoul playing with the farm, we can see the meanings they are actively making, in Gordon Well's sense. We can use their ideas. We need to talk to Hans in terms of his knowledge of cows through an advert. We need to talk to Raoul in terms of comparing the real field of cows with the television advertisement. The free-flow play shows us how each child is bringing together and integrating his knowledge of cows. In other words, we begin with the child. Bruner's Acts of Meaning (1990) begin with what we want the child to know about cows. We need to look at the child in order to gain the appropriate starting point. The emphasis is on breaking down knowledge as we prepare the child for adult life, and take him further into the culture.

Either way, free-flow play is important. The difference lies in whether the starting point is the child (Wells) or the content to be taught (Bruner). If we remind ourselves of the first chapter, and the three Cs of the curriculm, the order is child, in context and content. This book begins with the child, because it sees free-flow play as an integrating mechanism. However, there would be no argument between Wells and Bruner that the context is crucial, or that all three Cs – child, context and content – are essential in the curriculum. In our observations in the home corner (with the cows in the field, or wherever we target), if we use the 12 features of play as observation tools, we deal with all three Cs in the curriculum in a simple, straightforward way.

Supporting the child's free-flow play – the importance of context

Race, culture, gender, poverty, special educational needs

We have less influence over issues surrounding race, culture, gender, poverty, special educational needs, and the family environment of the child, than we do over the material provision we make in the classroom. The more we discuss, and ask parents about their own childhood free-flow play, the more we gain insight into the way it is perceived by each child's family. We need to strive to construct some shared meanings, as Minnie Kumria (1986) points out. We cannot, in reality, impose our views of free-flow play on parents. Children, after all, belong to their families, not to us. However, we can share our knowledge about free-flow play – for, as we know, parents do want the best for their children, but are not always clear about what that is. Wanting the best for children draws together parents from a variety of ethnic groups and cultures, parents of children with special educational needs, and professionals working directly with their children.

Basic provision

From Margaret McMillan onwards, early childhood workers have had to make do with under-resourced facilities. Those choosing to work directly with young children have always shown ingenuity in getting the most out of the resources available. The basic material provision we make is an example of this.

There are many books available which suggest imaginative ways of improving basic provision, and which help us not to leave out important aspects of it (Gregg, 1971; Matterson, 1989 and the wealth of PPA publications available).

(a) Easy to provide material

Some materials are relatively low cost – such as sand, water, clay, mud, homemade playdough, junk model material, offcuts of wood, scraps of paper, chalk, wax crayons, shells, pebbles, twigs, moss, offcasts for dressing-up clothes, etc. These have been the time-honoured basics since formal early years education began.

(b) Consumables

Other materials that are essential are glues, paints, paper, pencils, felt pens, sticky tape, string, nails, screws, etc. These are consumables, and need careful provision. It constrains children's possibilities to develop the technical prowess they demonstrate during free-flow play and rich representations if they do not have sufficient opportunity to manipulate and explore with these materials. There is a difference between allowing children to waste or damage materials, and helping children to explore and learn to become competent in using them, e.g. sticky tape. If we want to help free-flow play, we need to help children to use materials through direct and frequent firsthand experience with them. For example, Jody (six years) made a nurse's hat and wore it while playing hospitals. Segun (four years) made a cape which he wore as Zorro in his free-flow play. These props helped the children as they established the characters and themes of their free-flow play.

Traditionally, many classrooms, have workshop areas, which encourage children to mix their own paint, find and use appropriate glues, brush sizes, appropriate paper colour and size, etc. These areas can be gradually extended, as children are helped to use them responsibly. More experienced children then begin to help new children to use the areas.

Some rooms, if there is space, have double provision – this might include, say, red clay in the workshop area (like the one just described) and a clay table outside with white clay. In this way, clay can be used on its own, or tools can be added to cut and roll it, or feathers and twigs, etc., can be put in it. We should not be operating on the 'clay on a Monday' syndrome – clay with rolling pins: Tuesday, clay with knives to cut it: Wednesday, clays with twigs and feathers: Thursday, and plasticine: Friday (to make cleaning up for the weekend simple). Ideally, clay should always be available in the workshop, where children can use it according to their current thinking, feelings or interactions with others. The same logic applies to other provision. Some days, different areas can be highlighted through double provision, but in a more open-ended way – and certainly not in a way which denies access to other areas.

For example, Michelle (four years) had used clay on Monday. She went to the clay table on Tuesday and found rolling pins and cutters. She wanted a knife, like the one she had used on Monday. She was told that Monday they had knives, but today was rolling-pin day.

In contrast, Oteri (four years) had used clay the previous day on a table highlighting it as an activity. She had enjoyed sticking feathers and twigs in it, and had been pleased with the hedgehog she had made. The next day, clay was not highlighted, but she went to the workshop area, and saw clay. She took a lump to the junk area in the workshop, and made a beetle using sticks.

Michelle was constrained in developing her firsthand experience of clay. Oteri was able to develop in hers, and represented animals with it on two consecutive days. Double provision highlighted clay for her.

(c) Materials requiring more investment

Some materials are more costly, but not in comparison with a science laboratory in a secondary school. Having many plastic construction kits which are incompatible may not be as useful in the long term as having only one or two sets of the same type, but plenty of it. The same applies to wooden, stackable free-standing blocks, which have a long tradition in early years education (Guru, ed., in press, 1992, directed by Bruce). Careful consideration of 'sets' of anything, from jigsaws to cookery to woodwork tools, can determine whether equipment will have lasting value or not. Perhaps we can again take up Lilian Katz's notion of mastery *versus* coverage in education. It is better to experience fewer types of construction kits in depth, and to become highly competent in using them, than to experience a wide range of sets, but remain at an early level of competence through not having enough of them. When we say it is important to give children a wealth of experience, we need to remember that quality of experience is also a central issue in helping children to free-flow play.

Language and action in a free-flow play partnership.

We need enough equipment of a particular kind. We also need to buy non-consumable equipment which will have a long life, or can be cheaply repaired. Adults therefore need to have development plans which help them over time to build up equipment with a long-term view.

Examples of a supportive environment

It is entirely understandable that we often set out basic provision in ways which constrain rather than increase firsthand experience, because it is so pre-structured. We want to look well-organised. It makes us seem effective and efficient in helping children to learn and develop. The more we pre-structure in advance the way the child is to experience an activity (such as Jack when he had to make a fish using a template, and then decorate it using one material – milk bottle tops), the less the child can experience during the activity. In contrast, Oteri made a hedgehog and a beetle, using the beautifully organised and presented workshop to do so. The structuring was open-ended, and allowed her ideas, feelings and relationships to contribute to her model.

We might also pre-structure in a constraining way when we adopt a 'theme' or 'project' approach. Rigid adherence to a narrow theme, e.g. colours, can mean that for a whole week everything is yellow – paint, soap, bananas, etc. This quickly becomes a teacher-led and teacher-dominated approach, which takes little account of the child's ideas. It cuts across the child's thinking by imposing a theme thought up by an adult. For this reason, many teachers and nursery nurses prefer not to use themes. They use their observations of children as the starting point (EYCG, 1989, p. 14).

Open-ended provision is crucial to children getting the most out of the firsthand experiences we offer, so that they can find their own level in it. It is then our job to be able to observe, and through doing this, to see what help they need now and next, e.g. how to make the colour brown to paint the hedgehog, or how to choose between glue or sticky tape for the model's hinges on the door to a house, or how to cut and roll clay, or how to make a den. In other words, we need to teach these things directly, as we pinpoint the child's exact requirements. In supporting children's learning and development, and so paving the way for the free-flow play which occurs when children apply their learning, we need to offer beautifully presented, open-ended provision. This will include outings, visitors, interest tables and activities. We need to be good observers, so that we can seize the teachable moment (Alice Honig, lecture, Froebel Institute, 1990) and use it to support the child's learning and development.

Increasingly, the way we present our provision will arise out of these observations. Observation, and the recording of it, helps us to see what children need now and next. For example, Jason (three years) is fascinated by the water wheel in the water tray. He keeps splashing everyone and the floor. The teacher and nursery nurse decide he needs a larger experience of this, and introduce a water tray on the floor, a tea-urn with a rotating tap near the sink, buckets, jugs, and a hair-washing hose set. He spends one and a half hours deeply involved in rotating taps, spraying and sprinkling; filling jugs and emptying them with a splash. There are spare clothes for him to change into whilst having the experience, so that his home clothes are kept dry. As he has this experience, he finds a cardboard shoe box, and fills it with water. He is fascinated by the way it gradually disintegrates into a pulp. Having observed this, the next day, the staff put cardboard boxes outside near the paddling pool and he sits in one, then fills it with water. He has a wonderful time making enormous mounds of pulp and transporting these into jugs, filled from the taps on the urn and at the sink. His body language, expression, and the time he spends (again one and a half hours), indicate that this is a major experience. The staff accompany these actions verbally – 'You've made it slushy,' etc. He has more than covered the aspects of Science in the National Curriculum dealing with transformation of state.

Is anyone at home?

Debbie (three years) and Tracy (four years) are firsthand experiencing the sand. Debbie had been annoying staff because she kept transporting sand from the commercially made sand tray, and dropping it in heaps on the floor. They decided it was their problem, not hers. She was manifesting a Piagetian schema – transporting. The staff reorganised the sand area so that it was in the old home corner (which had high walls). They put a plastic sheet on the floor, and a 'beach' of sand was made, with shells and pebbles in it. They also put tip-up trucks, spades, buckets, etc., in the space. Now Debbie could transport without making adults fraught.

Sam (three years) keeps hitting children. Staff realise they cannot change his behaviour, which involves trajectories being explored. However, they can change the way he experiments with trajectories, as his present behaviour is unacceptable. Two boys and a girl (10 years) from the local primary school are invited to come in and demonstrate their fencing. They belong to a fencing club in the school. They made up a story involving three friends (like the Three Musketeers), and fencing comes into this as part of the story. A lunge pad is fitted in the playground, and under supervision using plastic swords, the primary school children teach some fencing moves. Sam willingly submits to the rules of the game.

Trajectories are also introduced in other areas, as staff realise that there are not many opportunities to use them in the activities offered. A pulley is introduced, involving trajectories up and down. It hangs from a girder in the ceiling, with a bucket attached. It is popular, and is less pre-structured than the lunge pad in the way it can be used. Sweeping leaves with a large broom, and mopping the floor, provide more trajectory experiences.

Another trajectory activity is organised, where small polythene bags are filled with water and thrown at a wall at the far end of the garden. When thrown hard, they splat against the wall, amidst shrieks of delight. This involves the firsthand experiencing of forces – 'Throw harder.' It also helps Sam to make cause and effect links. Both the pulley and the forces involve children in aspects of the Science programmes of study in the National Curriculum.

In a reception class with 30 four year olds and one teacher (who trained for the junior age range), Sandeep, Oteri and Min crawl in and out of the dressing-up clothes. These are hanging on a rack near the home corner. The clothes keep falling down, and the children delightedly crawl under them. The teacher's immediate reaction is to stop them: they are causing chaos. However, something from her own childhood – her own delight as a child in crawling under things – makes her hesitate before reacting crossly. She asks the children what they are doing. They are bunny rabbits in a burrow. She had thought her rendering of *Peter Rabbit* the previous day unsuccessful, and had vowed never to introduce Beatrix Potter to a whole group again. However, here were children taking up the idea of burrowing. She told them that she did not want the dressing-up clothes made messy, but when they had cleared the mess, she would help them to make a better burrow. She had old sheets and bedspreads and four old clothes-horses. They made a wonderful burrow, which took up aspects of the English and Technology programmes of study in the National Curriculum.

In all these examples, we have seen that easily provided materials can present rich and varied firsthand experiences for children. They are especially influential in creating the optimal context for learning and development, if they are planned in the light of our observations of children. It is also useful to remember our best free-flow play moments from our own childhoods. However, as Minnie Kumbra points out, we need to ask the parents of the children we teach to tell us about their childhoods, so that we are introduced to other cultures, and can be sensitive and reactive to the experiences of the families we work with.

Recording how we support children's free-flow play

Recording how we support free-flow play always needs to be part of our general recording. When we support children, we need to note:

(a) How basic provision helps free-flow play (e.g. painting, stories, climbing frame, home corner, etc.).

(b) How we help children with content (maths, dance, etc.).

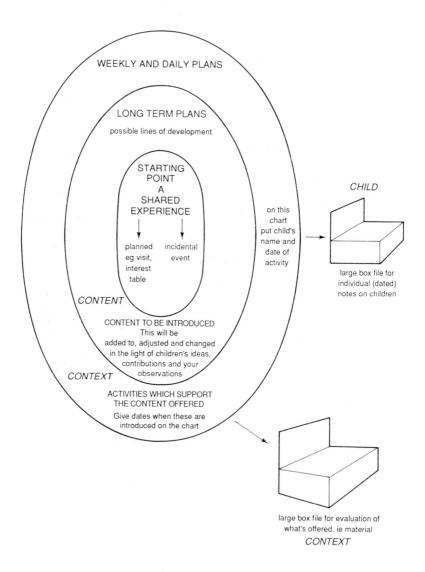

Figure 9(a)   The structure of the flow chart, and how it cross-refers to notes on individual children and evaluation of provision.

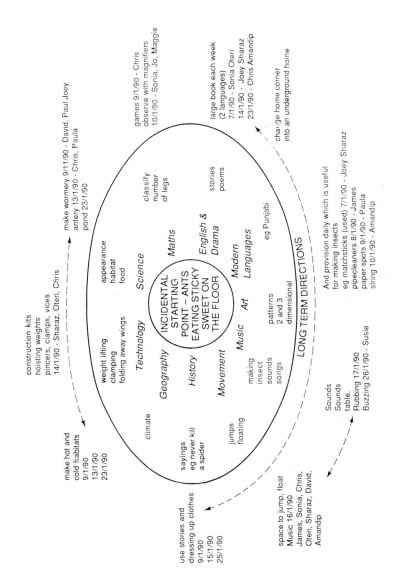

Figure 9(b)   Staff used this flow chart for three weeks. It could last for less or longer, depending on the children's use for it. Look to see what aspects of the National Curriculum have been offered. It is important to build on existing good practice if we are required to work with it. It should be an added resource to our work, if used this way

We need daily, weekly and long-term records of these. The long-term records will show our advance planning, and will indicate what Wynne Harlen calls 'possible lines of direction'. These will inevitably be added to, adjusted and changed in the light of our observations of the children.

The above flow chart developed out of a shared experience. In a nursery class, ants had made a trail into the classroom during the half term, towards a sticky sweet that had been left in the middle of the floor. Rather than clear this up on the Monday morning, the teacher and nursery nurse decided to leave it, and put chairs around it for children to have a good view. They found that most of the children were fascinated and wanted to sit and watch – some for 10 minutes or so.

Local Authorities are demanding long-term planning, as part of record keeping in educational settings – even with very young children. The more open-ended plans can be, the better chance children have of being in an environment supportive to their learning and free-flow play. The advantages of flow charts are:

1   They help us to think ahead about gathering equipment we might need, and about outings.

2   They give us a rough sense of direction, in offering balanced content in the curriculum.

3   They can be linked, by cross-referencing, to the individual notes on the children in the box files, e.g. the date when an activity is introduced can be put on the flow chart, with names of the children involved in it. The flow chart only tells us who chose to be present at an activity, but this is useful to know when reflecting on the experiences children have taken up. The individual notes might tell us more, depending on where we observed the child that day.

4   They can be adjusted daily and weekly to take up the current interests and developments of particular children. Activities and content can be added, or left without further development, accordingly.

5   They help us to work with colleagues as a team, precisely because we have to negotiate a shared direction. We are keeping each other informed as we change course, or sidetrack. We all know the reasons for

changes, and it makes us all focus on children's needs. Marian Dowling (1990) stresses that this must always be our starting point.

6 Flow charts help us to share our knowledge and understanding of free-flow play with parents. We can also ask parents to become involved by adding to them, changing them, or adjusting them. They reassure parents that something is planned and thought through, which may not at first be apparent. It is unreasonable to expect parents entering the classroom to have acquired the practised and trained eye of the early years practitioner.

3 Extending the child's free-flow play

In the last section, we saw the need for our basic material provision to be varied, open-ended, and reactive to current needs, as well as having the continuity and progression which comes from effective long-term plans.

The line between supporting and extending is fine. However, the examples in the previous section all used the familiar, basic provision known to the children. When we extend, we begin to use the familiar to take them into the unfamiliar. Alistair (four years) is playing with the dolls house. He has arranged the furniture with dolls round a table, eating a meal. He chats away, becoming different characters, and narrating in between. He wants a picnic. The dolls are trotted outside, and cups, food, etc., are spread out. It is not very satisfactory, because he is a child who needs props to support his free-flow play. The teacher finds a green cloth and spreads it on the floor. She makes a path of pebbles. She puts the smallest potted plants from the nature table on the green cloth. She puts twigs which look like trees into a base of plasticine, and places them on the cloth. 'What's that?', asks Alistair. 'It's my garden', she replies. 'You can play with it if you like,' – and she leaves him, so that she does not take over his free-flow play. He takes up the invitation, but rearranges the garden. It is a human need to make the territory we inherit our own by rearranging it. He returns to it the next day.

Alistair knows about using existing props. He does not know about creating them. His teacher has signalled how to go about this in his current free-flow play, and noted this in his individual record. One of the greatest problems of a heavily pre-structured classroom, either in the way activities are presented, or through narrow themes, is that it cuts across this possibility. It gives the message that there are particular ways of doing things. Everything else is wrong, or substandard. Didactic materials – commercially produced objects such as templates, or outlines – lead to didactic approaches, which cut across the creativity of extending free-flow play. The same applies to pre-structured toys (often misnamed 'educational'). Unless children are helped to extend into less familiar ways of using them, free-flow play is constrained. We saw how staff in a nursery school helped children to use My Little Pony and He Man in less familiar ways, through the introduction of the Pegasus story.

Segun (six years) loved to make paper aeroplanes, and enjoyed free-flow playing with them. His teacher showed him how to cut flaps to give the wings lift. He soon incorporated this new knowledge into his free-flow play.

Daisy, Galia and Ruth (seven years) were free-flow playing 'old-fashioned times' with the dressing-up clothes. There was a nanny, a fine lady and a servant. It felt slightly Victorian to the teacher. She made an interest table of Victorian lamps, bonnets, photographs, books, etc. She showed a video of a school's programme, 'How They Lived'. She helped the children make crinolines, using hoops from PE equipment. She encouraged them to convert the home corner into a Victorian house. The free-flow play increasingly demonstrated the knowledge being acquired of Victorian life. This was noted in the individual records of each child.

Summary

In this chapter, we have looked at practical strategies which help us to observe through the 12 features of play, support, extend and record children's free-flow play. This will mainly be through the bedrock of firsthand experience, extending material provision, and conversation with children, parents or colleagues, as cultural experience.

9 The Three Rs of Early Childhood Education

In this book, we have looked at the basics – the three Rs – of free-flow play. We have re-explored the meaning, principles and practical aspects of free-flow play. This has led us to re-state its importance in early childhood education. We have re-affirmed that it requires a central place in the early childhood curriculum. The three Rs of free-flow play are re-exploration, re-statement, and re-affirmation.

Re-exploration

Back to basics

The word 'play' is too broad to be useful, but has an important traditional place in the early childhood curriculum. In this book, Göncü's phrase, 'free-flow play' (1987), has been taken up, because it encapsulates the essence of play. The 12 features of free-flow play, have been culled from philosophical, theoretical and research literature, both past and present; and, from my own practical experience as teacher and parent, are crucial in identifying and building on high-level free-flow play.

In re-exploring 'play', through the narrowing down of the terminology, we can juxtapose free-flow play with other processes – likely precursors such as exploration, manipulation, discovery, and contemporaries such as games, humour, representation and decentration. This helps us to put free-flow play into a manageable and useful perspective, where it is not viewed in isolation from other aspects of the early childhood curriculum. The exact and precise boundaries and relationships of free-flow play with these other processes need further exploration and adjustment.

Free-flow play saves the child from being pinned down and constrained in development, and so enables children to operate at their highest levels and to integrate everything they know. Because it gives freedom and opportunity for this, free-flow play, in turn, enriches the more product-orientated aspects of development. The richer the free-flow play, the richer the subsequent products. The beneficial results will be seen in paintings, models, creative writing, dances, musical composition, mathematical thinking, etc. as well as in sports and games performances.

Re-stating the importance of free-flow play

The 12 features of free-flow play help us to re-state its value in the early childhood curriculum.

Feature 1   It is an active process without a product (Rubin *et al.*, adapted).

Feature 2   It is intrinsically motivated (Rubin *et al.*, adapted).

Feature 3   It exerts no external pressure to conform to rules, pressures, goals, tasks or definite direction (Rubin *et al.*, adapted).

Feature 4   It is about possible, alternative worlds which involve 'supposing' (Rubin *et al.*, adapted) and 'as if' Atkins 1985-8), which lift players to their highest levels of functioning. This involves being imaginative, creative, original and innovative.

Feature 5   It is about participants wallowing in ideas, feelings and relationships. It involves reflecting on, and becoming aware of, what we know – or metacognition.

Feature 6   It actively uses previous firsthand experiences, including struggle, manipulation, exploration, discovery and practice (Rubin *et al.*, adapted).

Feature 7   It is sustained, and when in full flow, helps us to function in advance of what we can actually do in our real lives.

Feature 8   During free flow play, we use the technical prowess, mastery and competence we have previously developed, and so can be in control.

Feature 9   It can be initiated by a child or an adult, but if by an adult, he/she must pay particular attention to Features 3, 5 and 11.

Feature 10   It can be solitary.

Feature 11   It can be in partnerships or groups, adults and/or children who will be sensitive to each other.

Feature 12   It is an integrating mechanism, which brings together everything we learn, know, feel and understand.

The following equation states the essence of free-flow play.

$$\text{Free-flow play} = \begin{array}{l}\text{wallowing in ideas,} \\ \text{feelings and} \\ \text{relationships}\end{array} + \begin{array}{l}\text{application of} \\ \text{developed} \\ \text{competence,} \\ \text{mastery and} \\ \text{control}\end{array}$$

Re-affirmation

Re-exploration of free-flow play has led us to re-state its importance, and so we can re-affirm its central place in early childhood education from the past, to the present and into the future. Indeed, its importance is so great that we can re-affirm the International Children's Charter (1989), which says that every child in the world has the right to play.

If the right to play is to become translated into practical reality, we need to do two things. We need to create oportunities to free-flow play, and – most importantly – we need to ensure that children have access to those opportunities. To do this, they need support and encouragement from adults to extend. We can re-affirm that all work and no play makes us pedestrian, dull and conformist. This is more serious than it sounds, for it is unlikely that our planet can survive dullness. The future requires the minds of those who have free-flow played: who have developed through wallowing in ideas, feelings and relationships, and who are technically proficient. We ignore this at our peril. We need to give children throughout the world their right to play. It is in the interest of adults, as well as of children, to do so. The older we become, the more difficult it is to learn how to free-flow play, especially if it is not part of our childhood memories (J. and D. Singer, 1990). We can get the most out of childhood, and take its benefits with us into adult life; or we can waste it, by filling it inappropriately, and dismissing free-flow play as something childish, to be left behind as quickly as possible. We need to remember we have only one childhood.

References and Bibliography

ALMY, M., MONIGHAN, P. SCALES, B. and VAN HOORN, J. (1984) Recent Research on Play: the Teacher's Perspective, in KATZ, L. (ed.) *Current Topics in Early Childhood Education*, Vol 5. USA: Ablex Publishing Corporation.

ARNOLD, C. (1990) 'Children Who Play Together Have Similar Schemas' – (Unpublished project submitted as part of the Certificate in Post Qualifying Studies).

ASHTON-WARNER, S. (1965) *Teacher.* New York: Simon and Schuster.

ATHEY, C. (1977), Humour in Children related to Piaget's Theory of Intellectual Development (p. 215–18) in CHAPMAN, A.J. and FOOT, H.C. (eds) *It's a Funny Thing Humour.* Oxford: Pergamon Press.

ATHEY, C. (1990) *Extending Thought in Young Children. A Parent Teacher Partnership.* London: Paul Chapman.

ATKIN, J. (1985-8) *Imaginative Play in Early Childhood Education.* OMEP updates, Vol. 1, pp. 67-9.

BAECE (British Association of Early Childhood) and The Pre-school Playgroups Association. A joint statement (undated) 'Four Years Old But Not Yet Five'.

BARTHOLOMEW, L. (1885) It's all very well in theory, but what about in practice? *Early Child Development and Care*, 19, 3, 237–51.

BARTHOLOMEW, L. (1989) Investigative Play, *Child Education*, May.

BENNETT, N. and KELL, J. (1989) *A Good Start? Four year olds in Infant Schools/*Oxford: Blackwell.

BISSEX, G. (1980) *Gyns at work.* MA and Eng: Harvard University Press.

BLAKE, MARY E. (1984) Reading in Denmark: A relaxed atmosphere is the key, *The Reading Teacher* (A Journal of the International Reading Association) Vol. 38, No. 1, October.

BLENKIN, G. and KELLY, V. (ed) (1988) *Early Childhood Education: A Developmental Curriculum.* London: Paul Chapman.

BODEN, M.A. (1979) *Piaget.* London: Fontana Paperbacks.

BRADBURN, E. (1989) Margaret McMillan. *Portrait of a Pioneer.* London: Routledge.

BREARLEY, M. (ed.) (1969) *Fundamentals in the First School.* Oxford: Basil Blackwell.

BREDEKAMP, S. (ed.) (1988) National Association for the Education of Young Children. Position Statement on Developmentally Appropriate Practice in Early Childhood Programme from Birth through 8 years, in *Young Children,* January.

BROWNE, N. and FRANCE, P. (1986) *Untying the Apron Strings.* Milton Keynes: Open University Press.

BRITTON, JAMES (1987) Vygotsky's Contribution to Pedagogical Theory. *English in Education* Autumn. (NATE).

BRUCE, T. (1976) A comparative study of the Montessori Method, and a Piaget-based conceptualisation of the pre-school curriculum. Unpublished MA dissertation, University of London.

BRUCE, T. (1978) 'Side by side. Montessori and other educational principles.' Montessori Society AMI (UK) Third Annual Weekend Conference, February.

BRUCE, T. (1984) 'A Froebelian loks at Montessori's Work. *Early Child Development and Care,* 14, Vols 1 and 2.

BRUCE, T. (1985) It's all very well in practice, but what about in theory?, *Early Child Development and Care,* 19, 3, 151-73.

BRUCE, T. (1987) *Early Childhood Education.* Sevenoaks. Hodder and Stoughton.

BRUCE, T. (1988) The Implications of the National Curriculum for Early Childhood Development, *TACTYC,* Vol. 9, No. 1, Autumn pp. 1–22.

BRUCE, T. (1989) Constructive Play, *Child Education,* May.

BRUCE, T. (1989) Play as an Integrating Mechanism, in *The Voice of the Child.* Conference Proceedings. OMEP London.

BRUCE, T. (1989) Parents as Partners. Guest Lecture; First International Outstanding Woman Scholar in Education. Virginia Commonwealth University, Richmond, Virginia, USA. The Link.

BRUCE, T. (1990) 'Only Playing'. Company Creche Magazine.

BRUCE, T. (1990) 'The Importance of Play'. PPA Journal.

BRUCE, T. (1990) Education with Care, in *The New Decade of Childcare.* BPW Seminar Proceedings, 31 May.

BRUCE, T. (1991) Play (in press) *Child Education.*

BRUNER, J. (1972) *The Relevance of Education.* London: Allen and Unwin.

BRUNER, J. (1980) *Under Five in Britain: The Oxford Pre-school Research Project.* Oxford: Grant McIntyre (Blackwell).

BRUNER, J. (1983) *Child's Talk: Learning to use Language.* Oxford: Oxford University Press.

BRUNER, J. (1990) *Acts of Meaning.* Cambridge MA: Harvard University Press.

CARLINE, SALLY (1988) Towards Dialogue in Young Children's Dance. Fourth International Conference. Dance and the Child International. Young People Dancing: London, Vol. 1 pp. 39–49.

CHUKOVSKY, K. (1963) *From Two to Five.* Berkeley, CA: University of California Press.

CITY OF SHEFFIELD EDUCATION DEPARTMENT (1986) *The Learning and Development of 3-5 year olds.* Schema.

CITY OF SHEFFIELD EDUCATION DEPARTMENT (1988) Dynamic, Vertical Schema, Thoughts, Observations, Resources.

CLARK, M. M. (1988) *A Survey of Research on Under Fives.* London: Gordon and Breach.

CLARK, M. M. (ed.) (1987) Roles, Responsibilities and Relationships in the Education of the Young Child, *Educational Review*, occasional publications, No. 13, University of Birmingham.

CLEAVE, S. and BROWN, S. (1989) *Four Year Olds in School: Meeting Their Needs.* Windsor: NFER-Nelson.

CLEVELAND TEACHERS (1987) *How Your Child Learns.*

COHEN, A. and COHEN, L. (1989) *Early Education: The Pre-school Years. A sourcebook for teachers.* London: Paul Chapman.

COHEN, D. (1987) *The Development of Play.* London: Croom Helm.

COHEN, S. (1966) The Problem with Piaget's Child, *Teacher's College Record.* No. 68 pp. 211–18.

COMMUNITY PLAYTHINGS (1981) *Criteria for Selecting Play Equipment for Early Education.* Robertsbridge, East Sussex.

CONOLLY, Y. (1983) OMEP; (World Organisation for Early Childhood Education) Conference, London.

CURTIS, A. (1986) *A Curriculum for the Pre-school Child.* Windsor: NFER-Nelson.

D'ARCY, THOMPSON (1961) *Form and Growth.* Cambridge: Cambridge University Press.

DAVENPORT, E. (1983) The Play of Sikh Children in a Nursery Class and at Home, *Educational Review*, Vol. 35, 2, pp. 127–39.

DAVIES, M. (1988) Of Secondary Importance and Primary Concern, Fourth International Conference: Dance and the Child International. Young People Dancing, London, Vol. 1 July pp. 69–78.

DAVIES, P. (1990) Chaos Frees the Universe, *New Scientist*, October pp. 48–51.

DEARDEN, R. (1968) *The Philosophy of Primary Education.* London: Routledge and Kegan Paul.

DEPARTMENT OF EDUCATION AND SCIENCE (1966) *Children and their Primary Schools* (A Report of the Central Advisory Council for Education). Vol. 1. London: HMSO.

DEPARTMENT OF EDUCATION AND SCIENCE (1988) House of Commons Education, Science and Arts Committee, *Educational Provision for the Under Fives*. London: HMSO.

DEPARTMENT OF EDUCATION AND SCIENCE (1989) Report by HM Inspectors on *A Survey of the Quality of Education for Four-Year Olds in Primary Classes*. DES Publications Despatch Centre.

DEPARTMENT OF EDUCATION AND SCIENCE (1989) *Aspects of Primary Education: The Education of Children under Five*. London: HMSO.

DEPARTMENT OF EDUCATION AND SCIENCE (1990) *Starting with Quality*. The Report of Inquiry into the Quality of the Educational Experience offered to 3 and 4 year olds. London: HMSO.

DEVON COUNTY COUNCIL (1990) *Young Children's Learning. A Curriculum for Three and Four Year Olds*. Exeter: Wheaton Publications.

DEWEY, J. (1938) *Experience and Education*. New York: Macmillan.

DITCHBURN, SUSAN J. (1989) Learning Revisited. University of Calgary, Canada. Conference Proceedings. *The Voice of the Child*. OMEP London, July.

DONALDSON, M. (1978) *Children's Minds*. London: Collins/Fontana.

DOWLING, M. (1988) *Education 3-5: A Teacher's Handbook*. London: Paul Chapman.

DOWLING, M. (1990) OMEP Humberside Conference.

DRUMMOND, M. J., PUGH, G., and LALLY, M. (eds) (1989) *Working with Children: Developing a Curriculum for the Early Years*. NCB/Nottingham Educational Supplies.

DRUMMOND, M. J. (1989) The Curriculum of Early Childhood, in ENTWHISTLE, N. (ed.) *Handbook of Educational Ideas and Practices*. London: Routledge.

DUNCAN, I. (1928) *My Life*. London: Victor Gollancz.

DUNN, S. and MORGAN, V. (1987) Nursery and Infant School patterns: sex related differences., *British Educational Research Journal*, Vol. 13, 3, pp. 271–81.

DWECK, CAROL. S. and LEGETT, ELLEN. L. (1988) A Social-Cognitive Approach to Motivation and Personality, *Psychological Review*, Vol. 95, No. 2, 256–73.

EARLY YEARS CURRICULUM GROUP (EYCG) (1989) *Early Childhood Education: The Early Years Curriculum and the National*

Curriculum. Stoke-on-Trent: Trentam Books.

ERIKSON, E. (1963) *Childhood and Society.* London: Routledge and Kegan Paul.

EVANS, D. (1978) *Sharing Sounds.* London/New York: Longman.

FEIN, G. (1981) Pretend Play in Childhood: An Integrative Review, *Child Development,* 52 pp. 1095–118.

FEYNMAN, R. P. (1990) *What Do You Care What Other People Think? Further Adventures of a Curious Character.* London: Unwin Hyman.

FIELD, T. and REITE, M. (1984) Children's responses to separation from mother during the birth of another child, *Child Development,* 55, p. 1308–16.

FROEBEL, F. W. (1887) *The Education of Man.* New York: Appleton.

FULGHUM, R. (1989) *All I really needed to know I learnt in Kindergarten.* Grafton.

GARDNER, D. E. M. (1969) *Susan Isaacs.* London: Methuen.

GARDNER, H. (1982) *Art, Mind, and Brain.* New York: Basic Books.

GARVEY, C. (1977) *Play.* The Developing Child series; BRUNER, J., COLE, M. and LLOYD, B. (eds). London: Collins/Fontana Open Books.

GERHARDT, LYDIA A. (1988) A Rationale for Development as the Aim of Dance in Early Childhood Education. Young People Dancing: An International Perspective. London DACI Fourth International Conference, Vol. 1, July, pp. 109–118.

GLEICK, J. (1988) *Chaos.* London/New York: Heinemann.

GOLOMB, C. and CORNELIUS, C. (1977) Symbolic Play and its Cognitive significance, *Developmental Psychology,* 13. pp. 246–52.

GÖNCÜ, A. (1987) Toward an Interactional Model of Development Changes in Social Pretend Play, in KATZ, L. (ed.) *Current Topics in Early Childhood Education,* Vol. 7 pp. 108–26.

GOODALL, J. (1990) *Through a Window: 30 Years with the Chimpanzees of Gombe.* London: Weidenfeld and Nicolson.

GREGG, E. and THE BOSTON CHILDREN'S MEDICAL CENTRE (1969–71) *What to do when 'There's nothing to do'.* Hutchinson/ Arrow Books.

GURA, P. (ed.), directed by Bruce, T. (1992). *Exploring Learning: Young Children and Blockplay.* London: Paul Chapman.

GUSSIN PALEY, VIVIAN (1984) *Boys and Girls. Superheroes in the Doll Corner.* Chicago: University of Chicago Press.

GUSSIN PALEY, VIVIAN (1985) *Wally's Stories.* London: Heinemann.

GUSSIN PALEY, VIVIAN (1986) *Molly is Three*. Chicago and London: University of Chicago Press.

HARDYMENT, C. (1984) *Dream Babies. Child Care from Locke to Spock*. Oxford: Oxford University Press

HARLEN, W. (1982) Evaluation and Assessment, in RICHARDS, C. (ed.) *New Directions in Primary Education*. London: Falmer Press.

HARLEN, W. and BLACK, P. (in press) Space Project. University of Liverpool.

HARTUP, W. (1983) Peer Relations in HETHERINGTON, E. M. (ed.) *The Handbook of Child Psychology: Social Development* (pp. 103-96). New York: Wiley.

HAZAREESINGH, SANDIP, SIMMS, KELVIN, ANDERSON, PATSY (1989) *Educating the Whole Child. A Holistic Approach to Education in Early Years*. London: Building Blocks Educational. (Save the Children)

HEBB, D. O. (1949) *The Organisation of Behaviour*. New York: Wiley.

HONIG, A. (1984) Working in partnership with parents of handicapped infants, *Early Child Development and Care*, 14, 1–2, pp. 13–36.

HOWDLE, L. (1980) Lecture Froebel Institute RIHE.

HUGHES, M. (1986) *Children and Number: Difficulties in Learning Mathematics*. Oxford: Basil Blackwell.

HURST, V. (1988) Parents and Professionals, in BLENKIN, G. and KELLY, V. *Early Childhod Education. A Developmental Approach to the Curriculum*. London: Paul Chapman.

HUTT, S. J., TYLER, S., HUTT, C., CHRISTOPERSON, H. (1989) *Play, Exploration and Learning. A Natural History of Pre-school*. London and New York: Routledge.

ISAACS, S. (1968) *The Nursery Years*. London: Routledge and Kegan Paul.

KAMII, C. and DEVRIES, R. (1977) Piaget for Early Years, in DAY, M. and PARKER, R. (eds.) *The Pre-school in Action: Exploring Early Childhood Programs* (2nd edition). Newton, MA: Allyn and Bacon.

KARRBY, G. (1989) Children's Concepts of their own Play, in *The Voice of the Child*. Conference Proceedings OMEP, London, July.

KATZ, L. (1987) Issues and Dilemmas in Early Childhood Teacher Education, in *Professionalism and the Quality of Caring*. Bristol Polytechnic Avon Early Childhood Organisation pp. 6–41.

KELLMER-PRINGLE, M. (1974:1980) 2nd edition, *The Needs of the Child*. London: Hutchinson.

KILPATRICK, W. (1915) *Montessori Examined*. London: Constable and Co.

KOESTLER, A. (1976) *The Act of Creation*. Danube Edition, Hutchinson.

KRASHEN, S. (1981) *First Language Acquisition and Second Language Learning*. Pergamon.

KUMRIA, M. (1986) Establishing co-operation between parents and staff: a parent's view, in BROWNE, N. and FRANCE, P. *Untying the Apron Strings*. Milton Keynes: Open University Press.

LEWIS, P. (1989) *Living With Differences. Religious Education*. London: ILEA.

LIEBSCHNER, J. (1985) Children learning through each other, *Early Child Development and Care*, 21, 1–3, 121–35.

LIVELY, P. (1987) *Moontiger*. London: Andre Deutsch.

LORENZ, K. (1963) Deterministic Non Periodic Flow, *Journal of Atmospheric Sciences* No. 20 p. 130.

MAIER, HENRY W. (1978) *Three Theories of Child Development*. New York: Harper and Row.

MASLOW, A. (1962) *Toward a Psychology of being*. Princeton: Van Nostrand.

MATTERSON, E. M. (1965; 1989) (3rd edition) *Play with a Purpose for Under Sevens*. Middlesex: Penguin.

MATTHEWS, J. (1988) The Young Child's Representation and Drawing, in BLENKIN, G. and KELLY, V. (eds.) *Early Childhood Education. A Developmental Curriculum*. London: Paul Chapman.

MCAULEY, H. J. (1990) Learning Structures for the Young Child: A review of the Literature, in *Early Child Development and Care*. Vol. 59 pp. 87–124.

MCKONKEY, R. (1986) Changing Beliefs about Play and Handicapped Children, in SMITH, P. (ed.) *Children's Play: Developments and Practical Applications*. London: Gordon and Breach.

MCKELLER, P. (1957) *Imagination and Thinking*. London: Cohen and West.

MCMILLAN, M. (1930) *The Nursery School*. London: Dent.

MEADOWS, S. and CASHDAN, A. (1988) *Helping Children Learn: Contributions to a Cognitive Curriculum*. London: David Fulton.

MEEK, M. (1985) Play and Paradoxes: Some considerations of imagination and language, in WELLS, G. and NICHOLLS J. (eds) *Language and Learning: An interactional Perspective*. London: Falmer Press.

MELLOR, E. (1950) *Education Through Experience in the Infant Years.* Oxford: Basil Blackwell.

MILLER, J. (1983) *Many Voices. Bilingualism, Culture and Education.* London, Boston, Melbourne and Henley: Routledge and Kegan Paul.

MILLAR, S. (1968) *The Psychology of Play.* Penguin.

MONTESSORI, M. (1912) *The Montessori Method.* London: Heinemann.

MOSS, P. (1988) *Child care and Equality of Opportunity.* London: HMSO.

MOYLES, J. R. (1989) *Just Playing? The role and status of play in early childhood education.* Milton Keynes: Philadelphia; Open University Press.

NASHIF, HUDA (1985) *Pre-school Education in the Arab World.* Beckenham, Kent: Croom Helm Ltd.

NAYLOR, H. (1986) Outdoor Play and Handicapped Children, in SMITH, P. (ed.) *Children's Play: Research and Developments and Practical Applications.* London: Gordon and Breach.

NATIONAL CHILDREN HOME (NCH) (1990) *Factfile: Children in Danger.* National Children's Home, 85 Highbury Park, London N5.

NFER SCDC report (1987) *Four Year Olds in School. Policy and Practice.* Slough: NFER SCDC.

NEILSSON, L. (1985) Letter in *Information Exchange*, September. Issue 14 Royal National Institute for the Blind.

NELSON, K. and SEIDMANS (1984) Playing with Scripts, in BRETHERTON, I. (ed.) *Symbolic Play*, pp. 45–72. New York: Academic.

NEWSON, J. and NEWSON, E. (1979) *Toys and Playthings. A Fascinating Guide to the Nursery Cupboard.* Harmondsworth: Penguin.

NICHOLLS, R. (ed.) (1986) Rumpus Schema Extra. Cleveland Teachers in Education (LEA).

NORTHAMPTONSHIRE SCHEMA WORKING PARTY (1990) *Finding Out More About How Children Learn.*

NUTBROWN, C. (1989) *Patterns in Paintings, Patterns in Play: Young Children Learning*, Topic 7 Issue 1 Spring. Windsor: NFER.

NUTBROWN, C. (1989) Up, down and round, *Child Education*, May.

OPIE, I. and OPIE P. (1988) *The Singing Game.* Oxford, New York: Oxford University Press.

OSBORN, F. and MILBANK, J. E. (1987) *The Effects of Early Education. A Report from the Child Health and Education Study.* Oxford: Clarendon Press.

PASCAL, C.(1990) *Under Fives in Infant Classrooms.* Stoke-on-Trent: Trentham Books Ltd.

PEASE, A. (1894) *Body Language: How to read others' thoughts by their gestures.* London: Sheldon Press.

PEN GREEN CENTRE FOR UNDER 5S AND THEIR FAMILIES (1990) A Schema Booklet for Parents.

PIAGET, J. (1962) *Play, Dreams and Imitation in Childhood.* London: Routledge and Kegan Paul.

PIAGET, J. (1968) *Six Psychological Studies.* University of London Press Ltd.

PIAGET, J. and INHELDER, B. (1969) *The Psychology of the Child.* London: Routledge and Kegan Paul.

PIAGET, J. (1974) *To Understand is to Invent.* London: Viking Press.

PIAGET, J. (1986) *Adaptation and Intelligence.* London: University of Chicago Press, Hermann.

PUGH, G. and DE'ATH E. (1984) *The Needs of Parents.* London: Macmillan.

PUGH, G. (1988) *Services for Under Fives: Developing a Co-ordinated Approach.* London: National Children's Bureau.

RICHARDS, C. (ed.) (1982) *New Directions in Primary Education.* Lewes: Falmer Press.

ROBERTS, M. and TAMBURRINI, J. (eds.) (1981) *Child Development 0-5.* Edinburgh: Holmes McDougall.

ROWLAND, P. R. (1990) Personal communication.

SESTINI, E. (1987) The Quality of the Learning Experiences of Four-year-olds in Nursery and Infant Classes, in *Four-year-olds in School: Policy and Practices* pp. 26–34 London: NFER SCDC.

SINGER, D. G. and SINGER, J. L. (1990) *The House of Make-Believe.* Cambridge, MA, London: Harvard University Press.

SMITH, F. (1985) Lecture, on Early Literacy. London: Institute of Education, University of London.

SMITH, LYDIA A. H. (1985) To understand and to help. *The life and work of Susan Isaacs* USA: Associated University Presses Inc.

SMITH, P. (ed.) (1986) *Children's Play: Research Developments and Practical Applications.* London: Gordon and Breach.

SMITH, T. (1984) Teachers and parents working together, in FONTANA D. (ed.) *The Education of the Young Child* (2nd edition) Oxford: Basil Blackwell.

SMILANSKY, S. (1986) *The Effects of Socio-dramatic Play on Disadvantaged Pre-school Children.* New York: John Wiley.

SPODEK, B. (1972: 1978: 1985) (3rd edition) *Teaching in the Early Years*. New Jersey: Prentice Hall.

STEEDMAN, C. (1990) *Childhood, Culture and Class in Britain*. Margaret McMillan, 1860–1931. Virago.

STEVENS, P. (1976) *Patterns in Nature*. Harmondsworth: Penguin.

STEWART, I. (1989) *Does God Play Dice? The New Mathematics of Chaos*. Harmondsworth; Penguin.

SUTTON-SMITH, B. (1979) *Play and Learning*. New York: Gardner Press.

SYLVA, K., ROY, C. and PAINTER, M. (1980) *Childwatching at Playgroup and Nursery School (Oxford Pre-school Research Project)*. Oxford: Grant McIntyre (Blackwell).

SYLVA, K. and LUNT, I. (1982) Child Development. A First Course. Oxford: Basil Blackwell.

TAMBURRINI J. (1982) New Directions in Nursery Eduction, in *New Directions in Primary Education*. Lewes: Falmer Press.

TAYLOR, D. (1983) *Family Literacy*. London: Heinemann.

TIZARD, B. (1984) *Young Children Learning*. London: Collins.

TIZARD, B., BLATCHFORD, P., BURKE, J., FARQUAR, C. and PLEWIS, I. (1988) *Young Children at School in the Inner City*. Hove: London; Hillsdale (USA): Lawrence Erlbaum Associates.

VYGOTSKY, L. (1978) *Mind in Society*. Cambridge MA: Harvard University Press.

WARLOW, A. (1977) Kinds of Fiction: a Hierarchy of Veracity, in MEEK, M., WARLOW, A. and BARTON, G. (eds) *The Cool Web: The Pattern of Children's Reading*. London; Sydney; Toronto; Bodley Head.

WATT, J., *From Nursery School to Primary School – A Symbolic Transition*. OMEP, Update Vol. 1 1985–8.

WEIKART, DAVID P. (1988) A perspective on High/Scope, *Early Education Research*, Vol. 33, pp. 29–40.

WELLS, G. and NICHOLLS, J. (eds) (1985) *Language and Learning: An Interactional Perspecive*. London: Falmer Press.

WELLS, G. (1987) *The Meaning Makers*. Sevenoaks: Hodder and Stoughton.

WHITEHEAD, M. (1990) *Language and Literacy in the Early Years*. London: Paul Chapman.

WILLIG, C. J. (1990) *Children's Concepts and the Primary Curriculum*. London: Paul Chapman.

WINN, M. and PORCHER, M. A. (1968) *The Playgroup Book*. Fontana/Collins.

WINNICOTT, D. W. (1971) *Playing and Reality*. London: Tavistock Publications (Also, (1974) Hammondsworth: Penguin Books.)

Index